Trusting YourSelf

How to Overcome the Psychological Barriers to Reaching Your Potential
Selling Life Insurance, Investments and Financial Planning Services

Sidney C. Walker

High Plains Publishing Co.
Denver, Colorado

Published by High Plains Publishing Co.
900 Lincoln Station Box 300786
Denver, Colorado 80203

This publication is designed to provide authoritative information in regard to the subject matter covered. It is not meant to be a substitute for hiring the services of a competent professional person when expert assistance is needed.

Editing Supervision by Patricia Patterson-Greeb
Formatting Supervision by Tom Raddemann
Cover Design by Robert L. Schram

10 9 8 7 6 5 4 3 2

Printed in the United States of America.

ISBN 0-9621177-0-6

Library of Congress Catalog Card Number: 88-82621

Dedication

To the courageous people who envision the ideal of how things can be and then risk trusting their intuitive instincts to bring that vision into reality.

Acknowledgements

I want to sincerely thank the following people for their contributions along the way: My wife, Jackie, for the courage to believe in me and dream with me. My parents for their ongoing unconditional love and support from day one. My friends whose belief in me has given me the strength to keep searching for answers, especially through the difficult times. Over one thousand clients who taught me well and helped me crystallize and internalize the information for this book.

Special thanks goes to the following mentors: To my manager in the life insurance business, Phil Kline, who years ago taught me the importance of asking the tough questions of myself and others. To Lynn Stewart for teaching me how to help others find their own inspiration and to face my worst fears so I could find my own. To Kurt Wright for so clearly demonstrating to me the power of purpose and the source of personal presence. To Gary Smith for his magical combination of consulting skills that have allowed me to quickly and painlessly resolve internal conflicts and continue to find my way past my illusions of limitation. To Tom Raddemann for teaching me his wizardry on the Macintosh and for the many late hours and weekends that it took to complete this project. To Judy Sabah for her partnership, technical guidance and the nudge of inspiration that I needed to write this book.

Contents

Preface - xiii
Introduction - xv
Notes to the Reader - xviii

Part One - Creating a Focus

1. **What Is Possible?** - 3
    Whatever You Can Imagine - 3
    What's the Catch? - 3
    A Success Story - 4

2. **Creating a Target** - 7
    You Get What You Ask For - 7
    What Do You Want to Get Out of Reading This Book? - 8
    Potential Objectives - 9
    Creating Your Own Objectives - 10

Part Two - How to Effectively Use Your Intuition

3. **How the Brain Processes Information** - 15
    One Piece at a Time vs. All at Once - 15
    Internal Mental Teamwork - 16
    Moving to a New Level - 17

4. **Knowing What Feels Intuitively Right** - 19
    Your Intuition as a Pathfinder - 19
    How Do You Know "What Feels Intuitively Right"? - 20
    Intuitive Experience Inventory - 21

5. **Obstacles to Knowing What Feels Intuitively Right** - 23
    It Seemed Like a Good Idea at the Time - 23
    Falling in Love with the Deal - 24
    If It Feels Good, Do It? - 24
    Only You Know "What Feels Intuitively Right" for You - 25
    "Check In" for the Best Answer - 25

6.   **How to Access Your Intuition** - 26
        Creating the Right Environment - 26
        Create an Alert Sense of Calm - 26
        What If You Don't Get an Answer? - 28
        Three-Step Summary - 29

7.   **Obstacles to Acting on What Feels Intuitively Right** - 30
        Yes, But What Feels Intuitively Right Doesn't Make Sense - 30
        What If You Know What Feels Intuitively Right and Don't Act? - 31
        One of Two Things Will Happen - 32
        The Fear of Disapproval - 32
        Simple Not Easy - 34
        This Is the Way We Have Always Done It - 35
        All the Experts Can't Be Wrong - 36

8.   **How to Practice** - 37
        Accessing Your Intuition Review - 37
        Hints for More Perfect Practice - 38
        Practice Situations - 38
        Intuitive Business Inventory - 41
        Signs of Progress - 43

Part Three - How to Effectively Use Your Vision

9.   **The Mechanics of Maintaining a Positive Vision** - 47
        The Difference Between a Goal and a Vision - 47
        Energize Your Vision by Your Belief - 48
        What Happens to Your Positive Vision? - 49
        Two Kinds of Visions - 50
        Where Negativity Comes From - 51
        You Are in Control - 53
        The Negative Spiral - 54
        You Need Positive Evidence - 55
        Letting Go of the Negative Evidence - 56
        Methods for Shifting Back to Positive - 57
        The Critical Moment - 58
        Double Your Money with Double Vision - 59
        You Can Change the Quality of Your Life in a Second - 59
        When the Going Gets Tough, the Tough Create a Positive Vision - 60
        The Impact of Vision on Your Intuition - 61

Part Four - Practical Applications

10. **Getting Excited About Your Work** - 65
    A Definition of Purpose - 65
    What Is Your Purpose? - 66
    Exercises to Establish Your Sense of Purpose - 67
    Use Your Purpose to Make the Right Decisions - 76
    Do What You Do Best - 76
    What You Do Best Inventory - 78

11. **Tips for Effective Goal Setting** - 80
    Control the Direction of Your Life by Setting Goals - 80
    Hunt for the Excitement - 80
    The Power of Visual Imaging - 81
    The Key to Long-Term Goal Setting: "Make It Up" - 83
    Regularly Update Your Goals - 85
    Affirming Your Goals - 85
    More Balanced Often Means Less Analytical - 87
    Artwork for the Subconscious - 88

12. **Overcoming Your Fear of Self-Promotion** - 90
    A Prospecting Discovery - 90
    Some Will and Some Won't - 91
    What Do You Say to Yourself After You Hear "NO"? - 92
    The Internal Conspiracy to Avoid the Unknown - 94
    The Accountant and the Adventurer - 95
    The Good News - 98
    Warming Up the Adventurer Mentality - 99

13. **Connecting with the Right People** - 102
    Trust Is a Must - 102
    Creating Rapport - 103
    Being Likable - 105
    Who You Are Being - 108

14. **Asking the Right Questions** - 110
    Who Would You Rather Work With? - 110
    Double Your Sales - 111
    Creating Emotional Leverage - 113
    What's in This for You? - 117

15. **The Spiritual Connection** - 119
    An Answer from Within - 119
    Trust in Something Bigger Than Yourself - 120
    Yourself or YourSelf? - 121

16. The Art of "Staying On A Roll" - 122
>   Key Concept Review - 122
>   You Will Be Tested - 124
>   What Is It Like to Trust Yourself? - 125
>   Little Things Make a Big Difference - 127
>   Don't Lose Your Marbles - 127
>   We All Benefit - 128

Appendices

Interview and Referral Tracks & Tips - 131
>   Tracking the Difference - 131
>   The Question-Based Initial Interview Track - 133
>   My Favorite Interview Questions - 136
>   Interviewing Tips - 138
>   Closing Presentation Format - 139
>   The Psychology of Getting Referrals - 141
>   Tips on Getting More Referrals - 142
>   Sample Language for Getting Introduced - 144
>   Sample Introduction Letter - 146

Closing Thoughts... - 148
Recommended Reading List - 149
About the Author - 153
For More Information - 155
Order Form - 157

Preface

A lot has changed in the financial services industry in the past fifteen years. The financial products available are more sophisticated, more numerous and ever changing. The significant factors that influence economic and investment trends are made readily available to us in the daily newspapers, on television and in magazines. More and more of us are becoming highly proficient users of computers which give us instant access to any information we want. The only limitation is our imagination.

The buying public is far more educated and is demanding to work with professionals who know what they are talking about from a technical standpoint. They want advisors who keep up on economic trends, new products and government regulations. They also want financial advisors who can consistently demonstrate that they will put the goals and priorities of their clients ahead of the opportunity to make a fast buck. The days of the quick sale based solely on the merits of a product without looking at the overall financial picture of the client are fast fading into the sunset.

Now, no matter how much you know about your speciality or how polished your sales skills are, you have to be a person who your clients can trust to take care of their financial needs and produce what they want and need. Whether or not prospective clients will want to work with you is determined not so much by what you know as by how people feel toward you and whether they trust your integrity.

There is only one way to come across as trustworthy. You have to demonstrate that you trust yourself. The purpose of this book is to help you fine-tune your ability to trust yourself. When you do, you communicate to others that you are the kind of person who can be trusted to consistently give them your best.

Some highlights of the things we will cover:

- The power of using your intuition to help you make better decisions in less time.
- How to know what feels intuitively right and to trust acting on those instincts.
- How to create a vision of what you want as a way to control the quality of what you get.
- How to overcome barriers to reaching your full potential.
- Rules to teach you how to trust yourself and how to have others trust you as well.
- How to get people to *want* to do business with you.

Introduction

My life has been an ongoing search for how to best realize my own potential. In the process of continually refining my strengths and evaluating their most appropriate use, I have developed a fascination and talent for helping people identify the emotional barriers that get in the way of reaching their full potential. Once the barriers are identified, I help my clients develop strategies to overcome those barriers using a process that is both empowering and immediately successful.

Like many other professional learners, part of my fascination with emotional barriers has been to resolve my own, and I have had an abundant dose of those to work through. Meanwhile, I have found the process of taking on my emotional barriers to be a great adventure as well as a great teacher. I have consistently found that there are a only a few things that we need to keep track of to maintain balance and success in life and that there are at least one million interpretations of what those few things are. Needless to say, it can get confusing. In the pages that follow, I will share with you those few things that I wish someone would have known how to tell me earlier in my career. I don't mean to say that people didn't try to tell me what I wanted to know along the way, they just didn't seem to have the right words or what they said didn't feel right to me. My hope is that the words and concepts in this book will fill in some of the missing pieces for you.

I regularly wear the many hats of peak performance coach, salesperson, seminar leader, speaker, consultant and "all purpose" counselor. I have spent thousands of hours working with hundreds of people individually as well as giving many seminars on progressive personal growth and development topics. I have worked with people of all ages in every occupation from Fortune 500 executives to hard rock miners. It's from this experience, along with the good fortune of having key mentors appear when I needed them most, that the information presented in this book has evolved.

I have always been intrigued with the dynamics of establishing quality human relationships in the business environment. As a result, I have gravitated toward occupations that require a high degree of technical knowledge along with the ability to be extremely effective at establishing rapport and getting people to take action.

You could say that most occupations fit this description to some degree. However, there is a group that is under extreme pressure to perform in these areas on a daily basis. These are the salespeople in the financial services industry selling life insurance, investments and financial planning services. The pressure is on because of the depth of the relationship required between salesperson and prospective client before any business is transacted. In other words, if the salesperson isn't adept at establishing a relationship of trust with the prospective client, he doesn't get paid. Furthermore, I have found that the financial services salespeople who have the greatest ability to establish a relationship of trust with their clients also have the greatest sense of trusting their own instincts and intuition or what I refer to as "trusting yourself." So for the better part of the past nine years I have been researching, observing and developing ways to teach people how to trust their intuitive instincts and enjoy the miraculous results and wonderful sense of self-fulfillment that come from mastering this skill.

In the process of coaching many financial services salespeople to trust their intuitive instincts, I made some important observations. I found that in order to consistently produce outstanding results, a very specific "mindset" had to be present in the salesperson. I discovered that almost every financial services salesperson could describe this mindset as a moment or a period of time when he felt like he was really at his best or "on a roll." I observed that for most of these salespeople, the mindset of "being on a roll" was an experience that would come and go. Once the mindset had disappeared, it was often very hard to get it back and appeared to be more a matter of luck than skill when it did come back.

Over time my goal became to take the element of luck out of being on a roll and develop a formula that would enable my clients to control this feeling and actually be able to create it on command. (It will come as no surprise to you that the title of my seminar program is The Art of "Staying On A Roll".) What I discovered was that the key to staying on a roll was to learn to trust your intuitive instincts or, more simply, to trust yourself. This book describes how to *create and control the mindset* that will allow you to consistently produce outstanding results simply by trusting yourself.

Does the program work and what have people been able to accomplish? First, let me say again that the information presented in this book has evolved from the "hands-on" experience of working with hundreds of clients and not from untested theories. I can very confidently say that there is nothing in this book that I have not used with consistent success both in my own life and with hundreds of clients. Second, when your skill is to help people determine what they are really excited about and what they will make a firm commitment to, and then show them how to maintain an inexhaustible belief in themselves, achieving the goal becomes the easy part. Furthermore, to a great degree, how successful people are with this kind of program depends on a combination of their imagination and their comfort zone. I have consistently witnessed that you can achieve any goal that fits who you most enjoy being and that feels intuitively right to you. Therefore, it is easy for me to be confident that my clients will achieve their goals if they have done their homework in terms of choosing the right goals.

How about measurable results? I have had many clients more than double their incomes in less than a year. Obviously that is a far more difficult task for someone who is already a leader in his specialty. There have been just as many success stories where the goal was to maintain moderate income growth, enjoy working more and free up additional time for more non-work activities. In all these cases, the key was learning the formula for trusting yourself and staying on a roll as opposed to the mechanical solution of trying to see more people in less time or trying to write bigger cases.

It is always gratifying to me when I have been able to help people get a barrier or two out of the way and have them reach their material goals in record time. My real favorites are when clients share with me the thrill of trusting their instincts and winning big in terms of both tangible results *and* self-fulfillment. This can be as simple as enjoying their business more because they have put some time and effort into making their style of doing business more empowering to them. Or, it is when they experience the excitement of closing a big case because they were "tuned in" to their intuition in an interview and that sensitivity closed the sale.

My hope is that this book will open the door to a level of awareness, happiness and self-fulfillment in selling financial services that you knew in your heart was possible, but needed the combination to unlock the door.

Sid Walker

Denver, Colorado

NOTES TO THE READER

In the stories and examples that I have related about my clients, I have changed the names to maintain confidentiality.

For simplicity, I have used the term "prospective client" throughout the book, realizing that you are most likely calling on clients as well as prospective clients. So please interchange "client" for "prospective client" where appropriate to your business.

For grammatical consistency and clarity, the pronouns "he," "his" and "him" have been used throughout instead of "she or he," "his or her," and "her and him." No sexual bias or insensitivity is meant.

Give yourself the gift of taking some quality time to read this book. Get in a calm, relaxed yet alert mental state and take your time. The information in this book is subtle, yet very powerful. I promise you the new level of effectiveness and self-fulfillment that is readily available will be well worth the time invested.

Part One : **Creating a Focus**

1. What Is Possible?

Whatever You Can Imagine

What is possible when you trust yourself? First, it is possible to get on a roll and to stay on a roll in all aspects of your life. It's also possible to feel a sense of purpose and meaning about what you are here to do. It's possible to consistently know what direction or course of action really feels right to you in any situation. You can develop a knack for knowing how to do or say the right thing at the right time and write more business than you ever thought possible. You can end each day with more energy and excitement about yourself and your career than when you started out in the morning. What some people call miracles (achieving what you want in life with practically no effort) become an everyday occurrence. In essence, whatever dreams you have about your financial services career are possible when you learn to truly trust yourself, and that is what this book is about.

What's the Catch?

"Sounds too good to be true," you say. "So, what's the catch?" Learning new skills is a process. It takes time, patience, determination and the willingness to make a few mistakes. It takes the ability to keep going one little step at a time, no matter how slow or fast it may go. I am sure you have had the experience of being about ready to give up on a project, and out of nowhere comes a breakthrough or an insight that causes everything to go together all at once. Learning to trust yourself is very much the same process.

It is about discovering, developing and learning to naturally be at your best the majority of the time. If you are dedicated and tenacious in your pursuit of this personally rewarding and empowering way of being, the path is easy to find.

In the process of learning to trust yourself, you may have to do more risk taking than you have done thus far in life; however, the payoffs are big. You feel more alive, more daring, have more fun and learn to care more about others as well as have others care more about you. You will have a more positive impact on the lives of the people who interact with you, and you will be able to let go of worry, fear, self-doubt, procrastination and self-criticism.

A Success Story

Ron, who is an investment broker, was referred to me by a client of mine. Ron was already in the process of establishing himself on a national level with a very wealthy clientele. He had already done extremely well in his metropolitan community and was specializing in a type of investment that was best suited to very large sums of money. Expanding nationally was the next obvious move.

When Ron and I met for the first time it was obvious that he was a highly skilled professional salesperson who knew the technical side of his business as well. He told me that he had seen a presentation given by a couple of his peers that had thoroughly impressed him. What amazed him was the level of confidence, charisma and the sense of competence that these men generated as soon as they walked into a room. Furthermore, these qualities became even stronger the moment they spoke.

"What I want is this ability to clearly radiate to others that I can be trusted and that I know what I am doing, the moment I walk into a room. Can you teach me how to do this?"

I understood the mechanics of developing that kind of charisma but I didn't have it laid out in steps, so I said, "I can help you under one condition: that I don't have to tell you exactly what we're going to do or how long it will take. We'll create the program as we go and after each session we'll determine if it feels intuitively right to keep going. I know we can create the feeling you want, but we'll have to create the process as we go and you'll have to learn to trust yourself more than ever. You'll have to learn to listen to your instincts and be willing to act on them starting now. Do your instincts tell you that my approach is right for you?"

Ron grinned and asked, "When do we start?"

Ron and I worked together for a couple hours once a month for about six months. He either taped our sessions or took notes, reviewed the material and thought it through. Then, when he was ready, he would call me for the next session.

Then one day something happened that let us both know how we were doing. Ron had an appointment with a very wealthy business owner in the Southeast, a man who had a reputation for being very hard to get in to see. Ron had a pretty clear idea of the "financial solution" he wanted to present to this man, based on information given to him by the firm's CPA. The numbers involved in this case, as well as the potential commissions, were extremely large, so the pressure was on. This sale would make a very positive change in Ron's lifestyle.

When Ron arrived at the meeting, the business owner, his chief financial officer, the CPA and the firm's attorney were all present.

The meeting started off with a couple minutes of small talk to break the ice. Then the business owner asked Ron to show him what Ron had prepared for him. At that moment, Ron's intuition told him to ask a few more questions to make sure he was on the right track before he presented his solution. This was risky since the proposal was based on information that the CPA had given him, and the business owner might object to further questions. Ron decided to trust his instincts and ask the questions anyway.

The business owner cooperated. After a couple key questions, Ron knew that his proposal was not the best solution given this new information.

Ron then said, "Based on this new information, I want to make a couple changes in what I have proposed." He explained why he thought a different course of action would be better suited for what they were trying to accomplish and that it would be easy to make the changes.

The business owner was quiet for a minute. Then he looked at his three advisors and said, "We can do business with this gentleman. I feel we can trust him and I think he knows what he's talking about. Let's do the deal. You fellows handle the details." The business owner then stood up, politely excused himself and left to attend another meeting.

Ron said the whole conversation took all of fifteen minutes. He knew he had gotten the deal because he was clear and confident within himself during that meeting and he had trusted his instincts to change his course of action midstream. The business owner sensed that Ron had the competence and courage to do what he felt was right and that he could be trusted.

Ron generated the feeling of trust in others because he trusted himself and his instincts. We celebrated over dinner and considered our program together complete and very successful.

The remainder of this book represents the highlights of a program that has evolved from working with hundreds of people like Ron. I hope that in taking the time to develop your instincts you will be rewarded as well as Ron was, both personally and financially.

2. Creating a Target

You Get What You Ask For

Jerry, an insurance agent who had been in the business for about ten years, had established himself as a leader in his agency and company. Jerry was intrigued by the level of success that I had obtained with a few of his peers, so he contacted me to see if I could help him increase his production level and consistency from month to month.

Several weeks after our initial meetings, I visited Jerry to see how he was doing. Things were going well, he said. He had sixty cases opened which were more than he had had at any other time in his career. "But," he added, "I can't figure out why I'm not closing more of them. I haven't made a sale in three weeks."

I asked Jerry what his current goals were and he told me that his goal had been to open thirty new cases each month--which he had done. I then asked him if opening cases was the only thing he had focused on and he said yes. Right then I knew what was missing. I then asked Jerry if he had an income goal for the month.

Jerry thought for a minute. Then he looked embarrassed. He suddenly realized that he had overlooked making a commitment to a monthly income goal. He had achieved his goal of getting thirty new cases opened per month; however, he had overlooked the most important part--getting paid for it.

In Jerry's ten years of experience, he had often had very successful months followed by low production months, but could never figure out why. He had achieved a level of success that many agents would have loved without ever committing to a monthly income goal. He thought that if he opened enough cases the money would take care of itself. On an annual basis it did, but not on a monthly basis. His sporadic record caused numerous financial problems during the low income months, but once Jerry began to commit to a monthly income goal, his production increased and stabilized almost immediately.

Keep Jerry's story in mind as we continue to discuss goals and objectives. Make sure that you are asking for all the key elements of what you want to achieve.

What Do You Want to Get Out of Reading this Book?

The following pages contain a list of objectives that I have helped many clients achieve. Also listed are some questions for you to answer that will help you get the creative juices flowing. Take a few minutes now to go through these exercises and identify as clearly as possible what you want to accomplish as a result of reading this book. Think big! What would be exciting and meaningful to you? Forget what anyone else wants you to do or thinks you should do and ask yourself, "What do I really want for me?"

Space has been left to allow you to do the exercises right in the book plus add any notes you wish. However, if you find that you need additional space, get out some paper and a file folder and start a file called "Trusting YourSelf," and I'll tell you why.

I once worked with a nationally prominent insurance and investment advisor to help him develop a more relaxed attitude toward his work. After several sessions together, I told him that I didn't think there was anything else that I could teach him that he didn't already know. He replied, "You're probably right, but I haven't been able to accomplish this on my own. What I'm doing now is creating new habits. I want you around until the new habits became a part of my routine."

I may not be able to "be around" in person as a reminder to you, but you can use this book and your notes as a way to remind yourself of the new behaviors that you want to create. So, whether you write in the book or use some other method to keep notes, you will want to review the information regularly until it becomes a part of you.

Focus your attention on what you want to accomplish in your business and how you would like each day to go if you could have the day go exactly the way you wanted it to. Your goals can be measurable, like a specific amount of income, or intangible, like a feeling that you want to have about yourself or your work. Both tangible and intangible goals are important. Be honest and creative about what you really want in your life. We'll talk more about how to set goals that excite you and that you can really commit yourself to in a later chapter.

The following is a list of objectives I took from my client files. Check any of them that apply to you and then answer the questions that follow.

Potential Objectives

- Accomplish more in less time so you have more free time.
- Make more of the right decisions in a shorter period of time.
- Have more fun with your work and your clients.
- Create a better balance between your business and your personal life.
- Substantially reduce "down" periods and increase your consistency.
- Get greater commitment from prospects and clients in less time.
- Increase your closing ratio.
- Overcome the fear or resistance to self-promotional activities.
- Eliminate any hidden barriers that keep you from reaching your potential.
- Increase your ability to "stay on a roll" for longer periods of time.
- Enjoy greater peace of mind and self-fulfillment from your work.
- Better understand what really motivates you.
- Set goals that you can commit to and reach.
- Feel a greater commitment and belief in your ability to achieve bigger goals.
- Experience greater happiness and control over your life.
- Increase your personal presence and get people to *want* to work with you.

Creating Your Own Objectives

To further define your objectives, answer the following questions:

- What do you want that you don't have now?

- What do you have now that you want to get rid of?

- What do you want more of in your life?

- What do you want less of?

- What do you want to feel that you are not feeling now?

- If you could wave a magic wand and change anything about your business or how you do business, what would you change?

- If nothing mattered, no one cared what you did, and money wasn't a restricting factor, what would you want?

Now take a few more seconds with each of the questions you have just answered. Go back and answer these additional questions for each question listed above:

How would you know if you had what you said you wanted?
What would be different?
How would it feel?
What would it look like?
What positive things would you be saying to yourself?
What positive things would other people be saying about you?

Add anything else that you can think of to make your objectives as real to you as possible. The more clearly defined your objectives are and the more they appeal to your five senses, the easier it will be for your brain to figure out how to achieve these goals.

Now, just for fun, imagine what it would feel like to have achieved everything you just said that you wanted. Take a moment to get that feeling. Would it be worth some time and effort to have that feeling all the time?

Part Two : How to Effectively Use Your Intuition

3. How the Brain Processes Information

One Piece at a Time vs. All at Once

You have most likely had some exposure to left and right brain theory, so I won't elaborate on this subject other than to examine how the brain processes information.

The most important difference between the left and right brain functions for our discussion is that the left brain is analytical and the right brain is intuitive. Generally, the analytical function has the ability to look at one piece of information at a time, while the intuitive function can look at all the pieces of information at once. For example, if you put three oranges on your kitchen table and you asked your analytical mind how many oranges there were, it would count "one, two, three" and then tell you three oranges. If you asked the intuitive mind how many oranges are on the table, it would look at the table and instantly "see" or "feel" three oranges without having to count them. In this way, the analytical mind "figures out" the answers to questions and the intuitive mind has an "instant knowing" or "intuitive feeling" of the answer.

Now you might say you can understand how the analytical mind can count the oranges and come up with three, but how can the intuitive mind know there are three oranges without counting them?

The functions of the brain are divided so that the analytical mind (or left side of the brain) collects information one piece at a time while the right brain (the intuitive side) takes that information and turns it into a feeling. The right brain, or intuitive mind, has its own special language which is intuitive feelings.

The intuitive mind takes the information about the oranges from the analytical mind in terms of what three oranges look like or feel like and then turns it into an "intuitive feeling" or "instant knowing." Notice the opposing yet complementary functions of the two minds--the analytical mind's ability to identify single pieces of information and the intuitive mind's ability to put many pieces of information together all at once into a single "intuitive feeling."

This leads us to the definition of an "intuitive feeling." An intuitive feeling is knowing in a split second something that represents a few bits of information up to millions of bits of information all processed at once. And, because the intuitive mind sees all the information available at once, there is no limit to the amount of information that we can process in a fraction of a second. As soon as you add more information, it becomes part of the "whole" or big picture that the intuition can monitor.

Internal Mental Teamwork

For example, one way we can see the intuitive mind at work is when we learn to do something that requires physical coordination. Remember how you learned to ride a bicycle? You probably had an adult there to help balance the bicycle while you got on it. Then you pushed forward on the pedal that was the highest from the ground, which started the bike to move. With your hands on the handlebars, you tried to steer the front wheel first to the right, then to the left, and you were off! What a thrill! You were on your own. Then you felt yourself begin to lean too far to the right. Suddenly you lost control and crash! You hit the ground hard, but that didn't stop you. With scraped knees and knuckles you said, "Let's try it again!"

While all that happened, your analytical mind worked quickly to collect, label and categorize all the little bits of information that had taken place, processing it for future reference. At the same time, your intuitive mind simultaneously took that information from the analytical mind and put it together into intuitive feelings that allowed you to do several things at the same time. Your intuitive mind collected and processed even more information from each attempt you made until suddenly you could balance yourself on your bicycle and ride easily with no conscious thought of all the steps involved. "Awesome" doesn't begin to describe this miracle that we take for granted.

Remember what it was like when you learned to drive a car, especially one with a stick shift? How about tying your shoelaces? Easy, right? It is now, but you fumbled through being a beginner while your analytical mind figured out the steps and your intuitive mind got the feeling for which combinations of actions worked and which didn't. Without the analytical-intuitive team within your brain, you couldn't do even the simplest things like get out of bed, walk to the bathroom and brush your teeth. We do these tasks without thinking about them now, but it took millions of pieces of information to learn them initially. We use the brilliance of the analytical-intuitive team in everything we do.

Moving to a New Level

Think of any complicated activity that you perform. With each one you jumped to a whole new level of skill or proficiency once your intuition got the feel of it. In typing or playing the piano, it was being able to feel and know where the keys were without having to look at them. In ballroom dancing, it's when you felt the flow of the dance steps and didn't have to consciously think about them. In tennis and golf, you moved to a new skill level when you watched the club or racquet face hit the ball rather than look to where you wanted the ball to go. In all of these examples, it felt risky to let go and trust the intuitive feeling rather than to consciously monitor every little detail.

In life and in selling financial services it's the same thing. We can learn to trust the feeling of our intuition and move to a whole new level of competence while developing skills and abilities that we had no idea we could achieve. With our intuition, there's nothing we can't learn to do and no limit as to how good we can be. Our intuition is always capable of going to a new and higher level.

It is important to realize the power of our intuition. We're not used to thinking of ourselves as the most powerful information processing center ever invented. We forget that through our intuition we have the capacity to process an unlimited amount of information all at once. Therefore, there is no limit to the potential of how good we can be except for the limitations we impose on ourselves.

Most of us have been taught to think of our intelligence as the sum total of what we learned in school along with what we've read or heard, combined with a few lessons from the "School of Hard Knocks." This level of limited awareness is the biggest barrier to achieving our true potential. The key to realizing your potential in the insurance, investment and financial services field is to rekindle the thrill of learning, not just out of a book, but being willing to "skin your knee" again.

Are you willing to take a couple spills to experience the joy and thrill of really being at your best? Would you be willing to get a little mud on your sleeve to learn how to be "on a roll" all the time? Would you be willing to trust your intuition and move to a whole new level of competence in all aspects of your life? If your answer is yes, then let's begin.

4. Knowing What Feels Intuitively Right

Your Intuition as a Pathfinder

The intuition needs a goal or a target to shoot for and a strong desire to reach that goal. Then the teamwork begins between the analytical and intuitive minds to create an intuitive feeling that will lead you to your goal. What this means is that if you have a goal in mind and a strong desire to achieve that goal, your intuition will start to work immediately to find the best path to achieve it. Intuition is like the rudder on a ship. It steers you toward your goal (the destination you have in mind) in the most effective and efficient way possible, using all the information you have at your command. The path, or course, that the intuition creates comes as something that "feels intuitively right."

Because your intuition deals with all the information from everything that you have experienced, it can see the best path to take to achieve your goal. When you trust your intuition you begin to sense when a particular course of action is right or not. It either "fits" or "doesn't fit" the path that your intuition has chosen.

Although intuition serves as a guide to lead you to the achievement of goals, the analytical mind is absolutely necessary to help you determine the best course of action to take. The intuitive mind could not function without the analytical mind's ability to label and organize each piece of information. But the analytical mind's perspective is too narrow to be a good navigator. It gets lost in all the pieces of information, loses sight of the goal and gets off on tangents. This is commonly referred to as "analysis paralysis." To overcome this condition, it's important to get in touch with your intuition in order to keep everything in its proper perspective and to achieve your goal in the shortest length of time.

How Do You Know "What Feels Intuitively Right"?

One of the required skills in using your intuition effectively is to be able to determine what feels "intuitively right." So how are we able to identify that feeling?

This is not an easy question to answer because there are as many ways of knowing what feels intuitively right as there are people. You will have to experiment to discover what this experience feels like for you. Let's explore some of the possibilities.

Remember that your intuition has the ability to see and feel millions of bits of information per second. It also has the ability to look at the course of action you are considering and tell you if that action fits or doesn't fit your long-term purpose and objectives. When a course of action fits or feels intuitively right, you have a sense or a knowing that it is right and that you are on target. Sometimes your intuitive answer will be a clear "yes" or "no" feeling. Other times the communication or signal from your intuition will be so subtle that you could easily miss it. Like every other skill, learning to hear or feel your intuition takes practice. Below are the ways a number of people have described this feeling to me:

"I feel it in my gut."
"I trust the feeling in my heart to tell me when something's right."
"It's a feeling I get in my head."
"It's something I feel in my heart and then hear it in my head."
"I just know. It is a sense of 'knowing.'"
"I consider all the facts, then sleep on it. I always know when I have the answer."
"I write down all the pros and cons and then ask my heart what to do."
"When something feels 'intuitively right,' I feel a sense of trust about it."
"I get the feeling, and then the words that come out of my mouth are 'I got it.'"
"I get the feeling of what feels right long before I know what the words are."

We're often forced to rely on our intuition when we don't have enough time to get all the information we would like or it's impossible to know all the details before we make a decision. Examples of this type of situation are demonstrated in the following questions. See if you can get a sense of whether or not the course of action you chose felt intuitively right to you at the time.

Intuitive Experience Inventory

Answer the following questions that apply to you.

- How did you choose your present home?
  What made you know it was the right place to rent or buy?
  Did it just "feel right" at the time?
  If your answer is yes, what did that feel like? If you weren't sure, what did that feel like?

- How did you know which career to pursue and which offer to take?
  Did the position "feel right" at the time?
  If your answer was yes, what did that feel like? If it was no, what did that feel like?

- How did you know who to marry?
  What sold you on your spouse?
  Was it a voice or feeling from deep within, or did you talk yourself into marriage?
  How does it feel when it feels right?

- Do you know fairly quickly when you are or aren't going to like someone?
  How do you know that? What does that feel like?

- Do you know when someone is going to buy your solution to their problem?
  How do you know that? What does that feel like?

- Have you ever been in an interview with a prospective client and all of a sudden you knew what to say and you risked saying it, even though you weren't sure it would work? It just felt right? And then your prospective client made a decision to buy shortly after that? When that information just came to you, what did that feel like? What made you trust using that information?

These are tough questions to answer concretely because the answers are usually tied up in subtle feelings that can be difficult to define in words. Take some time to really go over the above questions now. It's important to explore how you have made significant decisions in the past to get a sense of the feelings that have guided you and to become aware of how those decisions turned out.

Chances are in answering the above questions you found there were times when you knew at once when the thing or course of action felt intuitively right. At other times, you had to gather additional information and analyze it carefully until you felt comfortable enough to come to a decision.

When you look at these past decisions on major issues in your life, which did you rely on the most--intuition, emotion or analysis?

Did you talk yourself into the decision, or did you "feel" it through?

Did you pay attention to a "special inner feeling," or did you give more credence to your intellect and ignore a warning that something didn't feel "quite right"?

Did you get carried away with an emotion in any of those decisions without collecting the information you needed to make the best possible choice?

Chances are there was at least one incidence when you wished you had acted on what you felt was right at the time. We will deal more specifically with this problem in the following chapter.

5. Obstacles to Knowing What Feels Intuitively Right

There are several obstacles to trusting and taking action on what feels intuitively right. This is a very important step to master because it does no good to know what feels really right and not be able to do anything about it. Let's examine some of these obstacles and how to get around them.

It Seemed Like a Good Idea at the Time

One danger is making decisions based on analytical data alone without checking in with your intuition. I like to call this approach "It seemed like a good idea at the time." An example of this is when you have ample evidence that you should buy a new sportcoat. The salesperson has said it looks great on you. It's made of a special summer weave for coolness and has a sporty cut for summer casual wear. It's a perfect neutral color that will go with everything you own. More than that, it's on sale! What else do you need to know? It's perfect, right? Then why is there a subtle feeling in the back of your mind that you have ignored that keeps whispering, "It doesn't feel right."

Many of you, I'm sure, own one of these sportcoats or something like it and I'll bet that you have rarely used it, if ever. Why not? Because it doesn't fit who you are from your intuition's bigger perspective. If the sportcoat didn't feel right to your intuition in the first place, no matter how good a deal it was, you'll always find a reason not to wear it. In short, if your intuition doesn't like something, your analytical mind's rationale is no match for it.

Falling in Love with the Deal

A corollary to "it seemed like a good idea at the time" is "falling in love with the deal, and wanting it more than it wants you." This is when you mistake strong emotional feelings for intuitive feelings. Intuitive feelings are not emotions, yet sometimes it's difficult to tell them apart. But there is a difference. Imagine what it feels like to walk across a room. Not necessarily an emotional experience, was it? Now imagine yourself walking down the aisle of a church to get married or walking through a room full of people after you have been introduced to speak. Add some importance, significance or risk to an event and the emotions are right there with you.

If you suspect that your emotions may be getting in the way of knowing your intuitive feelings, *stall*. See if you have the same excitement about "the deal" after a good night's sleep. Time away from an emotionally charged situation helps you to clarify what is strong emotion and what is intuitively right. A telltale sign that emotion is fogging your intuitive sensitivity is when you don't want to wait until tomorrow, you want it now! In most cases, waiting until tomorrow isn't going to make any difference. If it looks as if you will lose the deal if you wait until tomorrow, then you have to convince yourself that this particular deal is so good that it could never come along again. I haven't found a deal yet that turned out to be that good but I certainly have jumped in on a few along the way. (What can I say? Love is blind.) On the other hand, what a thrill when your emotions are strong and what you really want to do also feels right on!

If It Feels Good, Do It?

Similar to "falling in love with the deal..." but a little different is confusing "what feels good" for "what feels right." When something feels intuitively right, you have a sense in your whole being that a particular course of action serves your purpose, goals and personality strengths and that it will contribute to your long-term objectives. What feels good, on the other hand, often is something that will provide short-term gratification but ignores the long-term implications. An example of something that feels good but may not feel right is to take the afternoon off and play golf or go to a movie and ignore issues that need your attention.

Consider your goals first and then ask your intuition if it feels right to take the time off. If it feels right, then do it. Many times what feels right will also feel good. But notice I didn't say, "If it feels good, do it." That can be a dangerous slogan when you don't check in with your intuition to see if your plan fits your overall purpose and long-term goals.

Only You Know "What Feels Intuitively Right" for You

Beware of the person who claims to know what is best for you, especially if you aren't sure yet yourself. Many well-meaning people will tell you what they would do if they were you. Well, they aren't you. We each have different backgrounds and different points of view. *No two people share the same reality.* You may listen to what they have to say, and they will have some great ideas, but only you can make the final determination on what feels right for you. This is not to say that you should never take anyone's advice. Just be sure you run it through your internal system and check it out with your intuitive self before you do.

"Check In" for the Best Answer

When making a decision, ask yourself: Does this course of action feel right? Then give your intuition sufficient time to come up with an answer. It may take a little longer to get an answer from your intuition's bigger perspective, but the wait will pay off in the long run.

6. How to Access Your Intuition

Creating the Right Environment

Your intuition by nature likes a quiet, peaceful, nonjudgmental environment. It takes its time to feel its way to the answers you seek. Like a great artist who works best away from negative stress or pressure, your intuition needs an environment free of negative criticism, distraction and interruptions. If you're like most people, however, your typical day at the office is far from being ideal and stress-free.

Create an Alert Sense of Calm

Stress is an inevitable fact of life. Since you can't always control the noise, distractions and pressures at the office, it is essential to learn ways to create this condition within yourself. The ideal state to access your intuition is best described as an alert sense of calm. There are several key elements that are necessary to help you achieve this state.

First, it is important to become physically relaxed and release any tension that you are holding in your body. Take a few slow, deep breaths. As you exhale, release any tension you feel. Stretch and relax first your arms, then your legs. Slowly turn your head from side to side, being very gentle with your neck. Close your eyes for a few seconds and think of something pleasant. This is a quick and practical way to get the tension out. If you have more time, you may want to do something more physical such as stretching exercises, a short walk or even a mini aerobic workout in your office. Not only will it help you relax, it will make you more awake and alert.

The second key element is to establish a positive mental vision or expectation for the immediate future. Make a conscious effort to be an optimist. Have faith in a power greater than yourself and trust that things will work out even though you may not know exactly how at that moment.

Next, you must have a specific goal or objective and make it as real in your mind as possible. An example of this would be to imagine your upcoming interview as a positive and rewarding experience for both you and your prospective client.

It is extremely important to have a positive vision and expectation of your goals because your intuitive mind will create a path for you to whatever you expect to achieve. The intuitive or subconscious mind makes no judgment about what material you feed into it as to whether it's positive or negative, large or small, etc. It accepts everything and works to bring about whatever instructions you feed into it through your conscious mind. If you are confident, prepared and expect to give a dynamic presentation, your intuitive mind will create the way for you. If you are apprehensive and expect to fail, your chances of failing are high. It's that simple. Your intuition will give you the most direct route to whatever outcome you choose.

The next step to accessing your intuition is to check in with it and ask it the questions you need answered. The irony of this is that it's so obvious we often overlook it. Simply stated, ask yourself what you need to know and your intuitive or subconscious mind will give you the answer you need.

For example, let's say you are in the middle of an interview and all of a sudden you're stuck and not sure which way to go. You can feel frustrated and keep talking, hoping eventually you will say the right thing, or you can relax, breathe deeply and create a positive expectation of what is to transpire. Then ask your intuition for the exact assistance you need and wait for an answer. The answer will come, although it may take a few seconds or so. This time can seem like an eternity, but consider this as a test of your faith in your intuition's ability to come up with the right answer.

You have to trust that your intuition will consider all the circumstances and give you the answer you seek if you are patient and listen carefully. Many right answers never materialize because people are in too much of a hurry to fill the silence rather than wait for direction from their intuitive minds. Once you feel you've gotten the intuitive answer, double-check it to make sure the direction or the approach fits the situation. Many sales are made or lost in these few seconds of waiting to feel the right answer.

It may sound as if it takes a lot of time to go through this process. In reality, it frequently takes seconds or less. Most likely you already ask yourself these questions part of the time now when you are "on," but chances are you are not doing it consistently, which means you are not consistently getting the results you want. Practice consciously checking with your intuition until you know what it feels like when you are really tuned in. When you have the right feeling, you can do most anything in a flash.

What If You Don't Get an Answer?

What happens if nothing flashes into your mind after you have waited? Don't panic. Most of the time your safest bet is to WAIT. There are several ways to wait or perform an "elegant stall." If you are in an interview, you can (1) say that you want to "give matters some additional thought" before you make a final decision on which direction would be best for your prospective client, or (2) give the ball back to your client by saying, "What are your thoughts at this point?" or "What are your feelings about this?" Many times I have found that when I got the prospective client talking, something he said triggered my intuition and I knew what to do.

I have also learned to respect a "no answer" communication from my intuition. Usually it meant that I didn't have a clear sense of what felt exactly right at the time. I needed more information or more time to process the information I had, or both. Because the intuition can see the whole picture, it can see what is missing and when I need to get more analytical data.

Simply stated, "no answer" is an answer. It means "wait" before you take action if at all possible.

Another possibility for not getting an answer at this point is that you did not really create an alert sense of calm with a positive vision (expectation) for the immediate future. You have to internally create the ideal conditions for the intuition to work before you will have much luck getting the answers you are seeking. As one of my clients aptly put it, "Your intuition is a lover, not a fighter."

Three-Step Summary

Let's summarize how to access your intuition:

1. CREATE AN ALERT STATE OF CALM:

PHYSICALLY: Relax. Release any tension you feel. Take a few deep breaths, stretch, do something physical that wakes you up and relaxes you at the same time.

MENTALLY: Create a positive vision or expectation for the immediate future. This is a sense of faith and trust that you will achieve your goals.

2. ASK YOUR INTUITION QUESTIONS:

Ask yourself the question that will give you the answer you need.

Double-CHECK the answer you get by asking your intuition if what you have heard or felt feels intuitively right for the situation you are facing.

3. IF YOU DON'T GET AN ANSWER:

WAIT before you make a final decision. You probably need more time and/or information, or you need to redo steps 1 and 2.

Learning how to listen to your intuition and being able to quickly sense what feels intuitively right can be a challenge. It takes time to learn to make the distinctions between the analytical, intuitive and emotional communications that we sense within. With patience and an open mind you can begin to make the distinctions between your different internal communications and learn to recognize and use them to their fullest potential. Now, let's examine a few of the more familiar internal communications that can get in the way of acting on what feels intuitively right.

7. Obstacles to Acting on What Feels Intuitively Right

Yes, But What Feels Intuitively Right Doesn't Make Sense

Being skeptical of your intuitive answer because it doesn't make total sense at first is a common occurrence. What feels intuitively right may not make immediate sense to your analytical mind. Your intuition may recommend that you do something that seems unrelated or out of step with the circumstances in which you are involved. This is only because you can't consciously see all that your intuition sees at that moment in time. Your intuition can see, hear and feel things that your conscious mind may not be monitoring. Have you ever thought of a person and within seconds they were calling you on the telephone? Or have you had the experience of meeting someone for the first time and had an instant rapport with them and later became friends? Have you ever been in a conversation with someone and felt as if you knew exactly what they were going to say just before they said it? These are all examples of the intuition's ability.

When what feels intuitively right doesn't make total sense, the best thing to do is determine what you have to lose if your perception is off. If you're in a situation where you have a lot to lose and you're extremely uncomfortable in taking the risk, this could be an example of having the right direction but the wrong timing. It could mean that some part of your plan still doesn't feel just right. In other words, if you know your direction is right but you're too scared to act, you need to find a smaller first step. If a smaller step isn't available, you have to ask yourself honestly if you are emotionally ready to deal with the potential consequences of that risk if there is an interim or temporary loss. You may need more preparation time to have the risk "feel intuitively right." At some point,

30

you will know whether or not it's time to risk what feels right, even if it doesn't make total sense. Then you take a deep breath, cross your fingers and trust in your intuition's ability to see the bigger picture.

Several years ago I was in the situation of having to choose where I was going to do a very expensive three-month training program to get some consulting skills that were very important to me. The program required me to spend about fifteen hours a week at the training location, along with several weekends. I could do the program in Denver or Aspen. The main difference between the two options was the four-hour drive to Aspen twice a week (which meant sixteen hours of driving time), the extra expense of gasoline, lodging and the extra time I would have to take off from work, which I didn't feel I could afford at the time.

The logical answer seemed to be to take the course in Denver where I lived. But no matter how much I thought about it, Aspen always felt intuitively right. I took an inventory of my potential losses and determined that I could handle them if my perception was off and I decided to trust my intuition. As it turned out, I had three of the most magical, wonderful months of my life, and I spent half the time in one of the world's greatest resorts. Plus, remember I said I didn't think I could afford to take the time off? Two days after I wrote the check to do the program in Aspen I had a large project come in that covered my income for the next four months. I called this good fortune a confirmation from the "bigger picture" that I had made the right choice.

What If You Know What Feels Intuitively Right and Don't Act?

What happens if you have an intuitive feeling and you don't act on it? For myself, as well as what I have observed with hundreds of clients, I've discovered that life is very patient and forgiving. But when we don't trust and follow our intuition, there is a price to pay and this is how we pay it. Whatever our current endeavors are, if they are not based on that gut-level feeling that lets us know we're on track with our long-term goals, our progress or success will fail in some major way over time to remind us that we are not doing what is right for us. The most common forms of payment are lost time, lost money, lost relationships and lost health. So even though it may look as if we are getting away with something when we avoid the risk of doing what feels right, the price we pay and the pain we suffer may be huge in the long run. Seeing this principle in action with hundreds of people, as well as in my own life, has made me work a lot harder to determine what is right for me and risk taking positive action a whole lot sooner.

One of Two Things Will Happen

This brings us to a very important premise in the effective use of our intuition. When we use our intuition to help ourselves achieve our long-term positive goals, one of two things will happen:

1. We get the results we wanted and achieve our goals, or

2. We learn lessons that are required to ultimately reach our goal.

The important thing to observe here is that we really can't lose. Remember that it's the intuition's job to show us the quickest, most effective path to our goals. A fascinating aspect about the intuition is that it doesn't see mistakes as negative occurrences. Rather, it sees them simply as required events along the quickest path to our goal. For most of us, correcting mistakes represents the turning points in our lives. Most people will readily admit they have learned more from their mistakes than from their successes. I recently heard part of a television program where they were interviewing successful entrepreneurs and asking them, if they could do it all over again what would they do differently? The answer that had the greatest impact on me was: "I would make more mistakes."

Ask yourself these questions:

- Would you be willing to trust and act on what feels intuitively right and make a few more mistakes in the process, if you knew for sure you would achieve all of your goals faster?

- How would you approach your life and work differently if you knew you couldn't lose?

The Fear of Disapproval

One of the most powerful forces that keeps us from acting on what intuitively feels right is the fear of disapproval. When we were children, we learned a very powerful lesson, which was that in order to survive (to be fed, loved and cared for), we had to get the approval of our parents or whoever was in charge of us at the time. If what felt right was in conflict with getting that approval, we most often chose to go for the approval rather than to be punished in some way. So we turned away from listening to our intuition and listened to what others wanted us to do in order to get their approval, because we thought we needed it in order to survive.

Unfortunately, we may still be caught up in that way of thinking today. We erroneously feel that the approval of others is the same as what feels intuitively right. Often they are the same for a long time. The conflict comes when we no longer find happiness or self-fulfillment in spending our lives trying to figure out how to get that approval. We begin to notice that this approach is not fulfilling and worse yet, all our hard work of trying to get approval is unappreciated. Our head says we need others' approval in order to survive, but our heart says we need to do what feels right in order to thrive. We start to ask ourselves, "Which is right?"

I'm sure you know from your personal experience that it takes a lot of work to resolve this kind of conflict in life and that you get tested on it regularly. What often happens is that you know deep within what feels intuitively right but you fear your course of action may be unpopular with the troops. So you opt to try for their approval and watch to see whether you get it or not. Then you put up with the hollow, disappointed feeling that comes from knowing what you really want and not acting on it. You may even begin to feel resentment toward those you are trying to please, even though you may care about them a great deal.

I worked with a financial planner named Jeff who had a dilemma. He had been pushed by a female business client and friend to take an awareness training class that she felt had been very beneficial to her. Jeff had wanted to please her because he liked her and she was one of his largest accounts. At a weak moment, he signed up for the awareness training even though he had reservations about it. She was elated and assured Jeff that he had made the right choice.

About two weeks before the awareness training program was to begin, I got a call from Jeff. He told me the story and said he was unsure about what to do. We talked for a while. I asked Jeff if the awareness training felt right for him, and he said no, it did not. Then I asked him if he would be willing to trust that his client would still want to keep him as her financial advisor even if he didn't take the training.

Jeff came back with, "What if she doesn't? I could lose a big account."

I then asked Jeff if their business relationship was built on his financial planning skills or his pleasing her every whim in order to keep her account.

Jeff didn't have an answer right then, but he called me back a couple days later. He said it was one of the hardest things he had ever done, but he gathered up the courage to confront his client. He told her that he was sure he would get value from taking the awareness training, but that it didn't really feel right for him at that point. His client said she understood and that she appreciated his honesty. Jeff still has the account today and has since told me that their relationship moved to a much deeper level of trust after the incident.

The main problem with attempting to please others rather than risking what feels intuitively right is that the results are rarely self-fulfilling. You are always left wondering what would have happened if only you had trusted yourself. The net result of attempting to get others' approval is that you become "other-centered," meaning that your satisfaction and self-fulfillment in life are dependent on something other than yourself. Sooner or later you will face an internal revolt against the lack of control and self-fulfillment in your life.

What do you do once the revolt begins? You can gain perspective by asking yourself the following questions:

- Are you happy with your life the way it is, or do you feel a calling for more control over your personal satisfaction and self-fulfillment?

- And if you chose the route of more control over your personal satisfaction and fulfillment, would you be willing to leave behind some people, places, things, habits and attitudes if you were called upon by your intuition to do so?

- Would you be willing to trust that what feels intuitively right is truly coming from a bigger perspective of who you really are, and that if you trust this part of you that somehow things will work out for the best for everyone involved?

Simple Not Easy

The challenge with the last question is that you can't readily see that things will work out for the best for everyone, including yourself. There are no guarantees. Plus, when you act on what feels intuitively right, your decisions and actions may not be popular with the people around you and they may tell you that you're making a big mistake. To go against what the significant others in your life have to say can be the test of a lifetime. You have to be willing to trust that your course of action is right for you and that somehow things will move to a higher level and you'll eventually be glad that you took the risk. The test period is the time between when you initially decide to take the plunge and the moment when you get some positive evidence that you made the right choice.

Don't let anyone tell you this is going to be easy, and some situations are easier than others. It definitely gets easier the more you trust and act on your intuitive feelings and when you see the long-term positive results.

Every time you trust and act on your intuition, keep a diary or log of the results. You will begin to very quickly see a pattern of positive results that will create the concrete evidence you need to keep trusting and believing in yourself.

This Is the Way We Have Always Done It

Another obstacle to acting on your intuition is the lure of mass consciousness. You've heard the phrases. "500,000 insurance agents can't be wrong!" Or "This is the way we have done it for fifty years." Or even, "It was good enough for my father and his father before him, so it ought to be good enough for you."

It takes courage to go against the agreement of large numbers of people, and to say, "I don't care how things have been done for the past fifty years, it doesn't feel right to me" and to act on your own convictions.

Have you ever heard that 20% of the people in sales make 80% of the money? Why do so few people become really successful?

It has been my experience from working with all levels of people in the financial services industry that the top 20 percenters (who live balanced lives) aren't really any smarter or better-looking. Furthermore, they really aren't more successful because their uncles were in the business before them and gave them hundreds of clients, and they don't work twenty hours a day seven days a week!

The major difference between the person who does "okay" and someone in the top 20% is that the top performers learn to consistently trust their intuition to tell them which direction to go, which products to sell, what types of clients to pursue, how to conduct an interview and when to take time off from work. By trusting their intuition, the 20 percenters develop and evolve a personal style that really fits who they are. This results in a much greater production level than that of the other 80%. The irony is that in many cases the members of the 80% group are putting in a similar effort but are simply repeating a limited set of skills that they learned when they first started their business. This is otherwise known as "the way it has been done for the last fifty years."

The theory has been to teach people how to survive first, then to let them figure out how to be a "pro" on their own. The problem is that once people are taught how to survive in the financial services industry, the desire to maintain the status quo of survival takes precedence over the risk of trusting their instincts and acting on what feels intuitively right. When this happens, many potential 20 percenters cut themselves off from their most powerful means for personal growth and reaching their real potential.

All the Experts Can't Be Wrong

"If all the experts say this is the way to do it, who am I to disagree because it doesn't feel right to me?"

Sound familiar? There are many stories about financial advisors who assumed that the experts knew more than *they* did and went against their intuitive instincts and lost money for their clients. The unfortunate part is that many times the financial advisors intuitively knew when something wasn't right about a particular deal. But because they couldn't explain their feelings in analytical terms, they decided to ignore their intuition and figured the "experts" knew what they were doing. It was a powerful lesson for those advisors when these deals lost money or fell apart in some way, when they knew something wasn't right from the start. It's wise to get the opinions of the experts. Then be an expert on what your intuitive instincts tell you and trust your instincts.

8. How to Practice

It's time to practice using your intuition. Your goal is to establish a greater level of competence and the ability to ask your intuition questions and get answers on what feels intuitively right to you. Before we get into some practice exercises, let's review the steps for accessing your intuition.

Accessing Your Intuition Review

1. CREATE AN ALERT STATE OF CALM:

PHYSICALLY: Relax. Release any tension you feel. Take a few deep breaths, stretch, do something physical that wakes you up and relaxes you at the same time.

MENTALLY: Create a positive vision or expectation for the immediate future. This is a sense of faith and trust that you will achieve your goals.

2. ASK YOUR INTUITION QUESTIONS:

Ask yourself the question that will give you the answer you need.

Double-CHECK the answer you get by asking your intuition if what you have heard or felt feels intuitively right for the situation you are facing.

3. IF YOU DON'T GET AN ANSWER:

WAIT before you make a final decision. You probably need more time and/or information, or you need to redo steps 1 and 2.

Hints for More Perfect Practice

LISTEN CAREFULLY to your intuition and be sensitive to very subtle, quiet feelings and thoughts. The communications from your intuition will be nonjudgmental and nonemotional. Remember, one way to test to see if it really is your intuition is to wait a minute or so, if that is possible. Then ask the question again to see if you get the same answer.

I have a psychologist friend who says that he always knows when his intuition is talking to him because he will have a thought that will seem to float out of nowhere, totally unrelated to anything he is doing at that moment. What he likes to do is then pretend to ignore the "intuitive communication" the first time and see if it comes back again. If it comes back a second time, he will act on it.

The key is to relax and have fun with this process. You will never force an answer from your intuition. It only performs under ideal *internal* conditions.

BE PATIENT. Intuitive feelings often take more time to get than analytical information. Remember that the answers are coming from a much bigger perspective, so allow your intuition time to retrieve the information and let it come through.

HAVE FAITH. Speaking from my own experience and from observing many others, I've found that your intuition is often testing you to see if you trust and believe in its ability. This is especially true if your intuition gave you an answer to a question yesterday and you didn't take action on it. A show of faith is extremely important to your intuition's willingness to give you more answers.

Practice Situations

The following are some examples of situations where you can practice retrieving answers from your intuition with minimal risk.

Sports

Sports (any physical activity really) are a great place to practice using your intuition. In most sports, your ability to do well is dependent upon how much you turn the control of your body over to your intuition and let it flow. No matter what the sport is, there is usually a way to slow down a little, relax the tension out of your muscles and let your body flow instead of trying to control its every move. Satchel Paige, the great baseball star, called it "jangling." When you "jangle," you let your whole body bounce loosely in a relaxed manner while you are waiting between pitches. When it's time to move, you can easily and quickly move in any direction. The reason this works so well is that it allows your intuition to sense all of your body so it can instantly react in the most appropriate way. And as you relax and move around in the rag-doll-type dance of the "jangle," it tends to balance the intuitive and analytical sides of your mind to allow you to "sense" much more of the action and intuitively know what is going to happen just before it happens. Professional tennis players have a similar technique. Watch closely when they are waiting for a serve. They each have their own little dance that keeps their intuition engaged and ready to respond appropriately in a fraction of a second.

Make an Agreement with Your Intuition for a Half Day

Most people find that when they start paying attention to their intuition, it sends them all kinds of messages in the course of a day about what to do next, who to call, who they should be getting back to, even when they should take a break and do something totally different.

Tomorrow at the beginning of the day, make an agreement with yourself that you will trust and act on your *intuitive messages* half the day and that your goal is to have an incredibly productive and fun day. Just keep checking in to see what you want to do next that feels intuitively right. See what you come up with. I guarantee the day will be more fun, productive, miraculous and fascinating. Then you have to decide if you want to have any more half days like this!

Pick Up the Telephone and Dial

One of my favorite intuitional games is to listen internally for who I should call on the telephone. I work with many clients and I have to trust my intuition to tell me when I should call certain people to "check in" and see how they are doing. With very few exceptions, when I have an intuitive feeling to call a particular person and then call them, they usually respond, "I was just thinking that maybe you and I should talk this week. I have a couple things I want to run by you." When you get an internal message to call someone, pick up the telephone and dial.

Interview with Your Intuition

You are in an initial interview with a prospective client. In addition to your usual questions, ask your intuition to tell you what questions you need to ask to really understand this client's motivations. The questions from your intuition will float quietly into your awareness. If the timing is right, ask the questions right then. Otherwise jot them down on your pad so you don't forget to ask them when the time *is* right. I have consistently found that the questions my intuition has come up with have gotten me the crucial information that I needed to close the deal. I am always amazed at my intuition's ability to see the bigger picture and sense the critical issues.

Ask Your Intuition Up Front

How about sitting down with the information after you have done an interview and are putting together the proposal? You can save a great deal of time and energy by asking your intuition up front, "My goal here is to have these people love what I show them and have them want to buy the solution. What approach feels intuitively right?"

After you get the direction from your intuition, put your analytical mind to work on finishing the details.

Use Your Intuitive Radar

In your next presentation with a prospective client, keep checking within yourself to sense any lapse of attention or interest on the part of your prospect. If you sense a signal from your intuition that something isn't right, stop whatever you are doing and ask your client, "How are we doing?" If you don't get a clear response that tells you what to do next, follow by saying, "It felt to me as if I might have overlooked something and I just wanted to see if that were the case."

Your prospect may not even be consciously aware that something wasn't right until you brought up the subject. Why not find out right then rather than get stalled or have to come back? You will be amazed at how your prospect's attention to you will increase and how his respect for you will grow after this kind of exchange. Most people are not used to having someone be that "tuned-in" to what they are saying and feeling.

Summary

In the middle of a presentation with a client, a subtle, quiet thought floats into your awareness that says something isn't quite right. Maybe your prospect sighed, or suddenly pulled back, or his facial expression changed and your intuition picked up on it.

Stop for a second and ask, "How are we doing?" If you get no response, follow with, "It felt as if I might have overlooked something. I just wanted to check in with you to see if that were the case."

Be sensitive as well as up-front with your prospective clients. It lets them know you're responsive to their needs and that you aren't trying to get them to buy something that doesn't feel right to them. By demonstrating your desire to fully understand them and helping them clarify what they really want, you will get the information you need to create a proposal that will feel right to them. And those are the proposals that people buy.

The following is an inventory of questions designed to get your intuition involved in fine-tuning the profitability of your business. Take some time here to get some additional practice using your intuition and put some money in your pocket at the same time.

Intuitive Business Inventory

Instructions: Answer the following questions, paying special attention to what feels intuitively right for you.

• If you could work with anyone, what market feels right to you?

- If you could choose the way you wanted to prospect for clients, what method(s) feel the most right for you?

- What type of relationship do you want to have with your clients? What qualities feel right to you?

- What questions can you ask your clients to better understand their needs and motivations? What questions feel intuitively right to you?

- Does what you are proposing to your clients feel intuitively right to you? Are you taking the time to find out what feels right to them?

- Do your plans for tomorrow feel right on a "gut level?" How about for the week, the month, the quarter, the year, the rest of your life?

- Do your plans for the next hour "feel intuitively right?"

- Does what you are doing right now feel intuitively right?

Signs of Progress

There are a couple things to watch for when you are practicing. If you have not consciously used your intuition very often in the past, you may experience periods of disorientation or confusion for a few days at a time. During this time you need to trust that positive things are happening internally while your mental system is trying to accommodate the new demands. Be willing to make what may seem like a few "stupid mistakes," and trust that your intuition is putting the pieces together as fast as possible to reach a new level of competency in the shortest amount of time.

If you feel disoriented or confused, you may want to postpone making any major decisions for a few days. As with any skill, when you move to a new and higher level there is usually a period of relearning and re-orientation to get through. The results are well worth the inconvenience for a few days while your internal system re-orients itself to its new capacity. The ability to be more, sense more and know more quickly what is really right for you and others is a skill worth cultivating. It will change your life!

As you continue to practice, you will notice your confidence building and you will want to take action on bigger issues and decisions. The beauty of working with your intuition is that it will tell you if it is too soon to make a move or if you need more information. You will learn to sense when it's time to jump in and risk. You will begin to intuitively know when the time is right.

Part Three : How to Effectively Use Your Vision

9. The Mechanics of Maintaining a Positive Vision

One of the key concepts for reaching your potential in the financial services business is how well you are able to create and maintain a positive vision toward achieving your goals. This skill is also extremely useful in eliminating down periods and increasing your consistency. Let's examine how to create a positive vision to quickly overcome barriers and thus achieve your goals more effectively.

The Difference Between a Goal and a Vision

There is an important distinction between a goal and a vision, although these words are often used interchangeably. A goal is something that is tangible and measurable in terms of quantity and time. If your goal is to talk to fifty (specific number) prospective clients per month (specific amount of time), you know with certainty whether or not you have achieved that goal.

A vision can be as simple as a goal or very complex as demonstrated below:

- A vision can be a single picture in your mind (snapshot) or it can be a series of mental images (like a movie).

- It can cover any amount of time from the next few seconds (immediate future), to a year, or even something that extends beyond your lifetime.

- Furthermore, you can work on several visions at the same time even though you may not be consciously aware of it. For example, you could be working toward a vision of what you wanted to have happen in the next hour, which could be part of a vision for what you wanted to accomplish during the week. That vision, in turn, could be a part of your vision for the month and so on.

- The most powerful visions are the ones that appeal to as many of the five senses (seeing, feeling, hearing, taste and smell) as possible. For example, it is much easier for the analytical and intuitive sides of your mind to direct you toward achieving a goal if you can both clearly see and deeply feel its importance.

Let's say that your goal is to earn an extra $1,500 so you can take a vacation to Hawaii in three months. Just thinking in terms of earning an additional $1,500 doesn't do much to help motivate you to go all out to achieve your goal. However, it would substantially enhance your ability to achieve that goal if you included all five senses like in the following situation:

...You are leaning in the teller's window at the bank while she is counting out $1,500 in traveler's checks as you mark off the last errand on your checklist. You are packed and ready to leave for Hawaii for the next ten days. You board the airplane with a good book to pass the flight time. Then you check into your hotel and change into your swimsuit and head out to a perfectly white beach with crystal clear, emerald green water. You order a drink and pick a spot on the warm sand where the warm water gently laps over your toes while you sip your cool, mildly sweet piña colada. You look up from under the visor of your stylish, new straw sunhat to see the hotel person rigging the catamaran that you have rented for the afternoon. The breeze is warm and steady. It's a perfect day for a sail...

As you can see, the vision I have just described is much more powerful than merely a goal of earning an extra $1,500 so you can take a vacation to Hawaii in three months.

Energize Your Vision by Your Belief

Once you have a clear vision of what you want to achieve, use as many of your senses as possible to set this vision in your mind. Then double-check to make sure your vision feels intuitively right to you. The next step is to turn that vision into reality.

There are primarily two things required to make your vision a reality. First you must give your vision the energy it needs to become real by *believing* in your vision. Believing is a persistent combination of imagining your vision as possible and worthwhile, along with staying in touch with the feeling of what it would be like to have your vision be real.

Once you have this vision clearly in your mind, ask your intuition for the best course of action for bringing your vision into reality. Then, step by step, the miraculous process begins of experiencing the events and circumstances that teach you what you need to know to achieve your vision.

There is usually a time lag or grace period between the time you create your vision and the time that the vision actually comes into reality or becomes physically real. Some visions take more energy in terms of belief and work to achieve, while others seem to materialize out of nowhere with very little effort. And in between is every variation you can imagine. This time lag can be frustrating when you want things to happen right away. Other times you are glad you had the extra time because you changed your mind about what you really wanted.

What Happens to Your Positive Vision?

Let's say that you have determined that your goal is to go on a week's vacation to Hawaii in ninety days. Also, let's say that you've determined that the additional money for your vacation has to come from increased sales. At this point, you may not be exactly sure how all the details are going to come together. This is a common occurrence when you are choosing goals that feel intuitively right because your analytical mind has not had enough time to figure out all the details. This is when you need to have faith in your intuition's ability to find a path to your objective even though it may be unknown to you at this point.

So you plan ahead and start taking steps in the direction of your goal. You make airplane reservations with your travel agency and mark the week off on your calendar.

A week goes by and things are going fairly well. You're working hard, writing new business, opening lots of new cases and you see the potential to have the extra money you need. Overall, things look good. Then you get some bad news: the air conditioning is out on your car and it's the middle of August. You have to get it fixed, and you didn't buy the extended warranty. It's going to cost you over $800.

Since other cash resources are not available at this point, you now have to earn $2,300 in order to go on the vacation. Now comes the real test of your goal and vision. Is this vacation something that you are really going to do or is it just a nice idea? *Watch what happens to your vision.*

Your first reaction is to call the whole thing off. You tell yourself it was a foolish idea to begin with. What business do you have in trying to take a vacation, especially to Hawaii? The timing isn't right. How are you going to be able to come up with an extra $800 when you were already stretching it for the $1,500? Plus, you now have to leave your car in the shop for a couple days and you need your car to do business. You're going to have to reschedule at least one important appointment. That's going to postpone getting paid on a large case that you needed to even consider risking the vacation. The evidence is getting overwhelming. You shouldn't go.

What has happened to your vision? Your positive vision has turned into a negative vision based on all the reasons (evidence) of why you can't or shouldn't go.

Then, somehow, the vision of sitting on the sunny beach with the warm water lapping over your toes floats back into your awareness and you say to yourself, now wait a minute! Let's not give up so easily just because of a few complications. You remind yourself that your business has actually been going very well. You have opened some excellent cases. Furthermore, you have a lot of business pending. Besides, you've got ninety days to make it happen! Here you were calling off the vacation because of some complications that showed up in the first week. Where is your faith and trust? What happened to your vacation goal and your vision of splendor on the beach? *Are you going to give up or change your vision every time there is a major complication or an obstacle?*

I'm sure you have experienced something similar to this example recently in some aspect of your life, and that you are familiar with the seesaw battle that can happen as you work toward accomplishing a goal. The real challenge is to see if you can maintain your commitment level and positive vision when you start to get tested by negative events and situations.

Two Kinds of Visions

There are other important aspects to notice about visions. First, there are two kinds of visions: positive and negative. The function of a positive vision is to add to your life in some way, while the negative vision takes something away. The quality of your dominant vision sends out a signal in every direction like a powerful magnet and pulls in events and circumstances that match that vision. Consequently, when your vision is predominantly negative, you will tend to attract negative things into your life. The same is true when your vision is positive. You then pull in positive things around you. Of course, every day has its combination of positive and negative elements. The key is that you can choose whether your vision is positive or negative regardless of what is happening to you. You have only to look at the quality of your life to determine whether you have chosen to create more positive or more negative visions. *The kind of vision you consistently choose, positive or negative, determines the quality of your results and how fast you will achieve your goals.*

If you could keep score for a day, giving yourself one point for every second you maintained a positive vision toward your goals and one point for every second you had a negative vision, what would your score be at the end of the day?

Many people have positive visions about half the time and negative the other half, and end up neutralizing their efforts after expending a lot of time and energy. The net result of this approach is to maintain the status quo and make no real headway toward achieving goals.

When I work with people who have a habit of equalizing their positive and negative visions, they always say, "But I am a positive person." There is a fascinating problem here in that many people don't know they are choosing to create negative visions *because they actually think it is positive to be negative*, or that you're supposed to be negative.

Where Negativity Comes From

Let's examine the attitude that negativity is positive and where it comes from.

One of the primary goals that we have as humans is survival. There is a part of our brain that is in charge of collecting information that maintains our survival at any cost. This part of our brain is very powerful. You can recognize its presence because it primarily thinks and speaks to us in terms of "what's wrong" or "what could go wrong." Our "survival mind" collects all the information it can about what's wrong or could go wrong based on our past experience. Once the survival mind sees some danger or what it perceives could be dangerous, it lets us know immediately so we can take precautionary measures.

Let me say again that the survival mind is very important. We could not survive long without it. The problem is that most of us overreact to what we perceive as danger, which causes all kinds of problems, as you will see.

To show you how obsessed we are with the "what could go wrong" mentality, think about how much of the daily news is about what's wrong. Ninety-five percent or more of the news focuses on disasters, because people have been conditioned to think that they need to know what's wrong in order to protect themselves from what could happen.

Excluding the weather, when is the last time you had to actually protect yourself from something that you heard about on the evening news? Again, excluding the weather, when was the last time that you actually changed your activities for the next day based on the "what's wrong" information you got on the news? But you do have a lot of precarious information about items such as murders, rapes, wars, assassinations, muggings, robberies, consumer fraud, deaths, plane crashes, car accidents and the latest diseases, just to name a few. Do you suppose that this regular dose of "what's wrong" information has an impact on your thinking, your attitude and your predominant vision for the day? You bet it does! How could it not have a powerful impact when we hear it every day, day after day?

On the same subject, let's examine some other examples. Think about the conversations that you have with people. What do you usually talk about? Is the conversation about "what is going right" or "what is of value" in your life, or is it about "what's wrong" or "what could go wrong"?

When you attend business meetings, is the dominant content of the meeting about all the wonderful things happening in the industry or about "what's wrong" with everything?

When was the last time you received a sincere compliment from someone? When was the last time you gave someone else a sincere compliment? When you think about your job, in general, you would probably describe it as being paid to figure out what's wrong with the situation and trying to fix it. Am I right?

It's important to see that negativity is deeply rooted in every corner of our existence and that it isn't going away. It's also important to hear that I'm not advocating that you totally ignore any information which may be important to your survival, safety and well-being. The key is to monitor how strongly you react to circumstances and events that could be considered potentially dangerous to your survival in some way. If you overreact and become unduly concerned about the impact of any event or circumstance, you will replace your positive vision with a negative vision. Then you will begin to give the negative vision the energy to become real by your belief in it. Your survival mind immediately generates its protective activity in response to this perceived threat. That's when negative things start to happen.

You Are in Control

An interesting relationship develops between the survival mind and the visions you choose. Whatever vision you choose to maintain, *positive or negative, the survival mind collects evidence to validate and support the predominant vision.*

If you maintain a vision of "having a productive day," the survival mind will look for evidence to support that vision. It will concentrate on what is right about the day or what is of value. The opposite was true in the example we used of the Hawaiian vacation. When your vision is negative, you essentially look for and collect all the negative information about what is going on around you.

It's important to see here that you choose and control whether you have positive or negative visions every day, all day. Therefore, you can control what type of evidence your survival mind collects, positive or negative. What this means is that you are creating your own reality moment by moment despite what events and circumstances are taking place around you. *How you choose to react to those events and circumstances in your life becomes your reality.*

The good news is that you can find the positive in whatever is happening and keep moving toward the achievement of your goals. Or, you can look for all the negative information and expend your energy trying to protect yourself from imagined situations that will most likely never occur.

We get so caught up in negatively overreacting to the things that happen or could happen to us, that we lose track of the fact that we are in control of how we react to the events and circumstances of life. And how we react moment by moment determines how effective we are at achieving our goals. The biggest challenge is to not panic when we are faced with negative circumstances and to not go into a protective or defensive posture. Things will only go downhill from there.

The Negative Spiral

Let's look at how we become negative from another angle. This is the negative spiral. The survival mind is on the alert, collecting its information to keep us alive and well and to validate our current positive vision. Then along comes a negative hit! You got only half the commissions you expected with extra bills that are due. Your vision instantly goes to negative and the survival mind moves into a protective mode. Your imagination begins to take inventory of what else could go wrong.

The following is an outline of the typical negative spiral:

1. Everything is going along fine with a positive vision.
2. Disaster strikes. You get only half the commissions you expected.
3. Positive vision of the immediate future turns negative.
4. You go into a protective-defensive mode, and begin looking for what else could go wrong.
5. Your survival mind continues to collect evidence about "what's wrong."

Minimal damage has been done up to this point. Fortunately, there is a time lag between when we first created the vision and the time it takes for the vision to become a reality. You can still shift back to the positive with minimal negative effects. But let's look at what happens when you don't and you let the negativity continue to escalate.

You may become self-critical or critical of others. You might begin to experience self-doubt about your competence and your ability to make things happen. You may worry about all the "terrible" things that *could* happen.

If you continue to hold a negative vision beyond this point, you will likely move into an "attack" or "withdraw" mode. This is where you find some reason to become irritated at the next person you meet, or you may want to get away from dealing with people altogether.

From here things can deteriorate very quickly into anger, resentment, desire to get even or a desire to run away from the situation. In extreme cases, the survival mind's strategy moves to things like zoning out in front of the television, overeating, drinking, drugs, social withdrawal, depression and finally health problems. The symptoms may not appear in this exact order, but you get the idea.

The price of a negative vision held over a long period of time can be devastating. Can you see the folly of maintaining a negative vision in the hope of protecting yourself from what appears to be wrong or dangerous out there? You may have the illusion that you are protecting yourself from potential danger on the outside, but in reality you are only slowly destroying yourself on the inside.

There is no way to win with a negative vision! All of that energy that we use to protect ourselves from what we fear might happen makes us miserable and in some cases seriously ill, and can even lead to terminal diseases. This tragic waste of human life can be totally avoided in a split second by a simple shift back to a positive vision.

You Need Positive Evidence

How do you change quickly from a negative vision back to positive? I have alluded to one technique already, which is to simply refocus on the positive like in the Hawaiian vacation example. That's a great technique when you can make it work for you and many times it will, but what happens those times when it doesn't?

Remember that the survival mind has been collecting evidence and reasons to validate your negative vision for a long time. How long you have maintained your negative vision, as well as how many times you have had it in the past, will determine how much negative evidence you have collected to prove that your negative vision is true. For example, if you have had a history of being weak in a particular area in your life in the past, you've probably collected a ton of evidence to back up that belief system. I mean you have proof! You can give examples, times, dates, places, circumstances, situations, witnesses, the whole works!

It is important to notice that while you were having your negative vision and collecting the negative evidence, you were ignoring the positive side of whatever was happening to you at the time. There is always a positive side about every circumstance or event in life no matter how negative it may appear at the time.

"Oh, come on now," you say, "How about death, how is that positive?"

Good question. Imagine what the world would be like if we just got old and didn't die. It would not be a pretty sight. Furthermore, taking care of all the old, incapacitated people would be the full-time occupation of everyone else who was fit enough to work. Everything wears out, which makes death a necessary and ultimately positive part of life.

There is a positive aspect to everything that happens in life if you look for it. Notice I didn't say it is always easy or obvious to find the positive or "what's right" aspect, but it's there. You have to trust that it's there and take the time to find it, especially if you want to be able to maintain positive visions.

Letting Go of the Negative Evidence

Instructions: Take time to consider your answers to the following questions and determine whether or not the ideas presented feel *intuitively* right to you:

- Maintaining a positive vision adds to life in some way, while maintaining a negative vision takes something away.

- You have the choice of either a positive or a negative vision moment by moment all day long.

- If you had the choice between collecting information that was going to add to your life as opposed to take something away, which would you choose to keep?

- Would you be willing to consider that all the negative evidence and information that you have collected while you maintained a negative vision was an overreaction and a logical mistake based on the way you were programmed to see the events and circumstances of life?

- Would you be willing to consider that the positive evidence or "what's right" information is what really allows us to thrive in life?

  (Sure, you still want to avoid potential danger, but this activity shouldn't preclude your ability to see the positive or "what's right" information that allows us to thrive.)

- Would you be willing to consider the negative evidence that you have collected as extremely hazardous to your ability to reach your potential?

- Would you be willing to let go of the significance that you have given this negative evidence?

- How do you think you would feel if you had only collected positive evidence about yourself from day one?

Now, let's begin to replace any negative evidence you have collected with positive evidence, especially about yourself. *To shift back to a positive vision, you have to be able to let go of the negative evidence you have collected about yourself, about others and about the situations you have been in.*

Methods for Shifting Back to Positive

The following is a list of methods that will increase your ability to shift back to a positive vision as quickly as possible if you are ready to let go of all the negative evidence you have collected during your negative visions.

TAKE AN INVENTORY OF WHAT IS POSITIVE or of value about the current situation (as opposed to "what's wrong"). List what is of value about you--your skills, your strengths, your mission, your purpose, your career, your accomplishments, your clients, your friends, your family, your spiritual relationship--whatever is appropriate. Find the evidence for why your cup is half-full rather than half-empty. By becoming aware of the positive aspects of any situation we generate the energy we need back into our systems. This happens when we reinstate a positive expectation for the immediate future.

SHIFT TO A BIGGER PERSPECTIVE that will reduce the significance of the current situation. Example: How important do you think this particular event or circumstance will be to you at this same time next year? Have you forgotten that mistakes are a required part of success in any endeavor? Remember, you need the lesson of the situation you are in to achieve your goals.

SHIFT YOUR PHYSICAL STATE by breathing deeply, doing a relaxation process or exercise (walking, running, stretching, working out). In the case of intense anger or frustration, find a private place and scream into a pillow or put a picture of the person that is driving you crazy next to the punching bag at the gym. Be creative; remember the quality of your life depends on your ability to shift to a positive vision right now. If you are having trouble shifting you may need to release some emotional energy in a safe way.

SEE THE HUMOR IN YOUR SITUATION. Laugh about your predicament, remembering that you always find a solution. Take the advice of the ancient Chinese proverb: To know is to laugh.

GET BUSY doing something that will give you a positive sense of accomplishment and divert your attention away from whatever is bothering you. Make sure you have a positive vision about whatever activity you choose to do.

TAKE A SHORT NAP OR SLEEP for several hours and let your subconscious work on shifting you back to a positive vision.

Once you have returned to a relaxed, ready state with a positive vision for the immediate future, follow the procedure for accessing your intuition and then determine what to do next.

The Critical Moment

There is a critical moment when you first notice a negative vision is forming. This is not a time to panic and begin to worry. That would only add momentum to the negative spiral. Instead, use the fact that you have noticed that you have moved into a "what's wrong" mode as a warning device that signals you to shift back to a positive vision. Having a negative reaction to negative events and circumstances is normal, but you don't want to overreact and maintain that negative vision if there is no real danger.

You can actually be more effective in a negative situation if you maintain a positive vision for the immediate future. I don't mean that you say "everything is great" when everything is falling apart. Instead you say, "I am faced with a negative situation here and I don't want to make it any worse than it already is. I trust that there is something positive that will come from this event even though I don't know what it is at the moment. I will maintain a vision of having this situation work out as positively as possible for everyone involved and trust my intuition to guide me to the best course of action in the meantime."

Double Your Money with Double Vision

We are in a constant state of being somewhere along the path to reaching our goals. In order to be effective, we have to be able to see and accept where we are now, and at the same time not lose sight of what we want to accomplish. Therefore, there are actually two visions to keep in mind: *where we are now, and where we want to be.* We'll use your checkbook to provide an example of how this works. You have to work with the amount of money that is actually in the checkbook in order to get it to balance and not overdraw the account. However, each time you use your checkbook, before you close the cover, create a positive vision of how much money you would like to have in your account. If all you ever see is the way it is now, you are not giving any energy to the more positive vision of the way you want it to be.

An easy technique to keep your bank balance building is to visualize an extra zero behind whatever numbers are there now just before you close your checkbook. For example, open your checkbook. In your mind's eye, add a zero to your current balance and imagine what it would be like to actually have that balance. What would it feel like? Determine an extra amount that feels intuitively right to you and every time you look at your balance see what is actually there and also see what you want it to be.

I have had many clients comment on the success of this technique. One client had this to say: "It is amazing how the technique of creating the vision of how much money you want in your checking account works. I was skeptical at first, but I kept envisioning a larger balance than what I had. After a couple weeks I noticed that money started to flow into my account that I wasn't expecting. It was a little here and a little there, but it started to add up! It was as if the moment I started to consistently imagine more money in my account, that somehow it started to find its way in there."

You Can Change the Quality of Your Life in a Second

As I mentioned earlier, visions can cover any length of time from the next few seconds to years from now and every amount of time in between. For example, when you begin an interview with a prospective client, you can create a short-term vision of how you would like the interview to go. When you are creating visions to enhance your ability to achieve your longer-term goals, you may be thinking in terms of greater periods of time like a week, month or quarter, or any longer amount of time.

I remember a discussion with a client who had a major revelation when he realized that he had limited his positive visions to just his long-term goals. Consequently, if several negative things happened to him in the course of a day, he typically developed a negative vision for the immediate future. He figured negativity was just something you had to put up with and went through the remainder of his day frustrated.

The importance of having a positive vision moment by moment hadn't occurred to him as a key to reaching his longer-range goals. We can't just have a positive vision about one point in time and expect the rest of time to take care of itself.

The most important span of time into the future is the current moment by moment or *the next moment of now*. Our entire lives are simply all the moments of now put together. Therefore, it's important to realize that the vision you choose to have in the next moment determines the quality of your life.

When the Going Gets Tough, the Tough Create a Positive Vision

Yes, you can control the quality of your life in seconds if you learn to quickly shift from a negative vision to a positive one. Of course, when things are going great, a positive vision is easy to maintain. The real skill is being able to maintain it when things are falling apart or when everything has gone wrong. That's when you need the positive vision the most and when it seems the most logical to be negative based on our prior programming. Be willing to change the logic of that prior programming by maintaining an unreasonably positive vision of the future when things are falling apart.

What often happens is that people will experience some negative event or circumstance that creates a negative vision. Then they maintain that negative vision until something positive happens.

Why wait until something positive happens (which may take awhile) when you can substantially speed up the process by simply changing your vision back to positive? This is one of the greatest sources of control that we have over life and also one of the most challenging skills to master.

The Impact of Vision on Your Intuition

Your intuition will find a path to your vision whether it's positive or negative. Sometimes people ask me if thieves use their intuition. Of course they do. Remember we have to use our intuition to perform the simplest functions.

A significant characteristic about thieves is that they have a negative vision which by definition means they will pull in circumstances and events that will "take away" from their lives. If they don't get caught, they will pay in many other ways for their negative vision. Some common methods of payment are loss of money, relationships, health and sense of well-being, to name a few.

We are all thieves when we maintain a negative vision. We rob ourselves of being everything we can be and of reaching our full potential.

Give your intuition a positive vision to work toward. Then trust and act on what feels intuitively right and you can't lose. With a negative vision, you can only lose, and from a much bigger perspective so does everyone else.

Part Four : **Practical Applications**

10. Getting Excited About Your Work

A Definition of Purpose

The single most powerful way to increase the enjoyment you get from your work is to experience a sense of purpose. With a sense of purpose, you feel a tremendously increased sense of personal satisfaction and self-fulfillment by feeling and acting in harmony with your intuitive self.

One of the reasons I enjoy working with insurance agents, investment advisors and financial planners is that these professions, in general, attract people who have a desire to establish meaningful relationships with their clients based on mutual trust, rapport and a sense of friendship. The emotional drive to establish these relationships and then help people creatively solve financial problems is the driving force for many people in the financial services industry.

Of course, no two of these people have the exact same sense of purpose because we are all different and occupy different points of view. However, many people are drawn into the profession because of a similar sense of purpose. So let's examine this drive to establish meaningful relationships to help us understand what purpose is and how it is different from goals and visions.

One of the unique aspects of a purpose is that it is ongoing. It's like going east. No matter how far east you go, there is still more east to go. If your purpose is to establish meaningful relationships based on mutual trust, rapport and a sense of friendship, this gives you a sense of direction. It doesn't tell you how many relationships to establish or in what period of time. Once you make that purpose measurable in terms of time and quantity, it then turns into a goal. For example, if you determine you will establish fifteen meaningful relationships based on mutual trust, rapport and friendship every month of this year, you have set a goal.

A purpose is much like a visual image in that it involves all the senses. The big difference between a visual image and a sense of purpose is the magnitude of the purpose. A purpose is so big it can wrap its arms around all the visual images you could create. A sense of purpose joins together and aligns every aspect of your being, including all the millions of pieces of information and experience that make up your personality, goals, desires and ambitions. To know your purpose, or experience a sense of purpose, is to know and feel who you are and what you are here to do.

What Is Your Purpose?

Since a sense of purpose is a feeling that includes millions of pieces of information and experience, it can be very complex and multi-faceted with the potential for many different interpretations. Also, because a sense of purpose is a feeling, it can be represented by a symbol which could be a word, group of words or anything else that would allow you to label the feeling. Some symbols are going to evoke a stronger feeling of your sense of purpose than others. This is why it is important for you to create your own experience or feeling of purpose. A set of words that may have a very profound effect on you and instantly bring forth a feeling of your sense of purpose may not do much for somebody else. I have found that as I mature and develop, my sense of purpose remains the same, but the words I use to describe it change over time.

Because a sense of purpose is essential to a feeling of well-being and to setting the right goals, I have included several exercises to assist you in beginning to define your own personal sense of purpose. Take time to complete these exercises. For the best results, keep asking yourself for the answers that feel intuitively right to you.

Exercises to Establish Your Sense of Purpose

PURPOSE EXERCISE 1 - INTERNAL DRIVE INVENTORY

Goal: to determine your strongest internal drives in words that create a strong feeling.

Instructions: Go through the entire list and circle all the items that give you strong positive feelings. Then go back and pick the top three or four *themes* that have the greatest feeling or meaning for you. Remember there are no *correct* answers and the meaning of each word or phrase is for you to determine.

personal achievement

happiness

earning money

being loved, being accepted

loving someone (others)

popularity

competence

independence

risking

being different and still fitting in

being your best

reaching your potential

finding excitement

being a leader

learning, gaining wisdom

gaining mastery

making a worthwhile contribution

fully expressing yourself

becoming an expert

making a positive difference

developing people or things

seeing how much you can get away with

winning

finding the good in others

gaining recognition

building something

gaining the approval of others

creating something

getting things done

doing good

dominating

being unique

being the best

gaining security, safety

controlling

having fun

working hard

having influence over others

experiencing life to its fullest

seeking adventure

power, authority

prestige

increasing effectiveness

waiting until the last minute

(If a word or phrase comes to mind that isn't on this list, please add it.)

PURPOSE EXERCISE 2 - INTERNAL DRIVE HISTORY

Instructions: In the space provided, list at least one accomplishment in each age category listed below that gave you the greatest sense of joy. These are accomplishments that you personally felt good about regardless of what others thought at the time. In addition to listing these accomplishments, answer questions 1-3 to further identify the important aspects of each. (If you don't get an answer to a question right away, don't dwell on that question. It probably doesn't apply to your situation.)

Approximate Age Categories

0-12
13-17
18-22
23-30
31-40
41-50
51-60
61-

1. What was the activity?
2. What did you actually do?
3. What specifically was the sense of joy?

Then, after you have listed the accomplishments in each age category and answered questions 1-3, go back and answer the following questions a-d for each accomplishment:

a. What abilities were demonstrated by this accomplishment?
b. What was the general subject matter?
c. What were the circumstances?
d. What were the relationships to other people and things?

SAMPLE ANSWER: 0-12 age category

Accomplishment: Alternate captain of championship ice hockey team

1. Team house league ice hockey
2. Demonstrated an intuitive sense for playing the game. Demonstrated leadership and good decision-making ability under pressure.
3. Feeling of recognition for being someone people believed in to make good decisions.

a. leadership, popularity, make decisions under pressure, knowing what is appropriate, fair
b. questioning judgment calls, penalties, rules
c. recreational, organized, indoor, team sport
d. closely related and dependent on others, strong feeling of friendship and sense of family

Age Category 0-12

Age Category 13-17

Age Category 18-22

Age Category 23-30

Age Category 31-40

Age Category 41-50

Age Category 51-60

Age Category 61 and Greater

After you have completed the above, please answer the following summary questions:

S1. Throughout your life, what activity has consistently produced the greatest sense of joy?

S2. What skills or abilities do you most like to perform?

S3. What do you most like about yourself?

S4. What patterns, trends or consistencies do you observe in your answers thus far?

PURPOSE EXERCISE 3 -
DESCRIBING YOURSELF "ON PURPOSE"

Goal: to create a description of what you are like when you are demonstrating your purpose.

Instructions: Complete the following in as much detail as possible:

What are you doing when you experience the greatest sense of self-fulfillment?

Who are you being when you experience the greatest joy?

Describe the visual images you see when you are being this person.

Describe what it feels like to be this person.

Describe the things you say to yourself when you are being this person.

Describe the conversations you have with other people when you are being this person.

Devote some time to these important questions and review your answers periodically to make additions or deletions as you discover new and important parts of yourself and your sense of purpose.

PURPOSE EXERCISE 4 -
WRITE YOUR STATEMENT OF PURPOSE

Goal: to create a set of words that causes you to deeply feel what your life is about.

Instructions: Take the information from the above exercises and use the combination of words and phrases to draw up a statement of purpose that has the strongest meaning and deepest emotional feeling for you. Don't worry about the statement being grammatically correct for now. Your statement of purpose could have as little as one word or as many as is necessary to create a strong emotional feeling deep within. The key is to come up with a definite theme that best describes the driving force in your life that you can review regularly and that provides you with a strong emotional charge each time you read it.

Use Your Purpose to Make the Right Decisions

One of the most important uses of your purpose statement and sense of purpose is that it gives you a clear sense of direction and a way to test whether a particular course of action feels intuitively right or not. In this way, your sense of purpose becomes a target for your intuition. If you are in touch with your sense of purpose and you ask your intuition for "what feels intuitively right," the answer from your intuition will lead you toward fulfilling your purpose.

The procedure is this. When you are presented with an opportunity that requires you to make a decision, whether it be business or personal, you simply ask yourself these questions:

"Does this opportunity feel like it is aligned with my purpose?"

"Does it feel like it will contribute to my overall sense of well-being?"

"Does this opportunity feel intuitively right?"

If your answers to these questions are "yes," you can pursue the opportunity knowing it is "on purpose." If the answer is "no" in any way, you will want to wait before making a decision pending additional information. Another possibility could be that the opportunity doesn't fit your sense of purpose at that moment and you may conclude that, although the opportunity is possibly very worthwhile, it doesn't fit at this time in your life. It may sound time-consuming to go through this mental process when making decisions. However, you will be surprised at how fast you will know if something feels intuitively right or not with a little practice.

Do What You Do Best

When I begin working with clients, I find out what they really enjoy about their work to help them determine their sense of purpose and develop a sense of what feels intuitively right for them. Then we develop strategies to make sure they transfer those powerful feelings into their workday.

Warren was thirty years old and had been an insurance and investment advisor for six years with a major company. He had a sales process that he liked and it produced excellent results for him. In fact, Warren had the kind of production that many others would love to have, but he wasn't satisfied. Warren wanted to grow and do better. He wanted to be a leader in his company.

When Warren and I first met, he told me that he had experienced several down months and seemed to have lost his energy and wasn't sure why. As we talked, I found out more about who he had worked with and what kinds of cases he had been writing. Most of his cases were family-oriented instead of with business and professional people. When I asked Warren how he was doing with his current prospecting, he said it wasn't going very well. This surprised me because Warren said he was good at getting referrals and had a large client base.

Then Warren told me that he was going after a different market. He had decided that if he was going to be a leader in his company, he was going to have to call on business owners and professional people.

I said that was okay, if that was the market he really wanted to work with.

Then Warren confided that he was really not comfortable with business owners and professional people. Half the time he felt intimidated by their level of education or their financial success and he was not relating to them well.

I then asked Warren the magic question. "Warren, would you be willing to be a leader in your company and not call on business owners and professional people?"

He looked at me like a little kid that just got a new bicycle for Christmas. He asked, "Do you really think that's possible?"

I assured him that it was and that he would have more fun and energy doing the things he loved to do and had already been successful in doing. He agreed to leave the glamour to the others for now. His specialty was the "Ma & Pa" market that he loved, and he was going to do more of it than ever before.

This conversation took place about two years ago. Last year Warren wrote over 150 cases and during one month he was one of the top ten agents nationally out of a total of 5,000 agents. I have seen many careers practically take off overnight when people finally gave themselves permission to do what felt intuitively right in the first place and put everyone else's good ideas aside. Some of the most successful salespeople I know in the financial services industry specialize in working with the "little guy." They enjoy that type of person. They get lots of referrals. They write a ton of business and they are leaders in their companies. And guess what happens to some of those "little guys"? They turn out to be "big guys" down the road.

I have also done a lot of work with the opposite group--the salespeople who live for the big cases and that is all they do. The challenge with this group is to stay "fired-up" about the amount of prospecting they need to do in order to get the few big cases. The financial pressure and the number of "no's" can be overwhelming if you don't have a strong sense of purpose to keep you going in the face of a lot of negative evidence. You have to be very good at maintaining a positive vision and finding the little successes each day since it's common to be busy and yet potentially have months go by without a sale.

Whether you make several hundred sales per year or you make ten, you have to decide what approach fits your strongest sense of purpose and feels intuitively right for you. Any approach or focus that falls short of having the feeling that "This is really me!" or "This is the way I am supposed to be doing this business!" is going to fail in some major way to remind you that you are off the mark. Why not take a few minutes now and ask yourself the following questions to find out how close you are to doing your business the way you really want to do it, in a way that taps your sense of purpose and that feels intuitively right for you?

What You Do Best Inventory

• What part of your work do you enjoy most?

• What aspect of your work gives you the greatest sense of accomplishment?

• What aspect of your work are you the best at?

- What prospecting approach has consistently been the most successful for you in the past?

- What were you doing when you were having the most fun with your business?

- What types of people are you most comfortable with?

- How would you describe the values of those people?

- What part of the business brings you the greatest sense of joy and accomplishment?

Are you spending the majority of your time and energy doing the specific activities with the kinds of people you listed above? If not, you should be. Streamline, delegate or eliminate anything that isn't on your list from the questions above. I guarantee you that it's worth your time and energy to make a few changes to allow you to spend more time doing what you love to do, the way you love to do it.

11. Tips for Effective Goal Setting

Control the Direction of Your Life by Setting Goals

Although we cannot predict with absolute certainty what is going to happen in life, it makes sense to utilize any means of control that we have over how things will turn out for us. One of the most effective ways we can help control our lives to some degree is to set specific goals. When we commit ourselves to a goal, a process begins that teaches us how to reach our goal. The goal then becomes a target for our whole being. The intuition then uses what it knows and reaches out to learn what it needs to know in order to obtain that goal in a way that is best suited to each of us.

When we set goals and make those goals a priority in our lives, we actually create a subconscious guidance system that will steer us to success. When we don't set clear goals, it doesn't mean life won't have any meaning or direction. It simply means that there will be a lot of confusion, frustration and *wheel-spinning* because the internal energy and resources will not be as effectively and efficiently focused. It is like the old saying, "If you aren't sure where you are headed, you may not get anywhere."

Hunt for the Excitement

We have discussed the importance of making sure the goals you set and commit to are "on purpose" and "feel intuitively right." Only the goals that have these qualities will give you a true sense of personal satisfaction and self-fulfillment. Once you have qualified your goals as being on purpose and intuitively right, there is yet another criterion to use as a test to see if you have the right goal--*excitement*.

About three years ago, I was doing a session with a very successful client named Brian who had won every award that his company had to offer. He had even set some records of his own for which they had to invent awards!

Brian called me because he was not feeling motivated and was having trouble coming up with goals for the new year. As we talked I realized that Brian had set goals repeatedly throughout his life and that he had consistently reached them in both his business and personal life. My diagnosis was that he was bored with the process of goal setting in the traditional sense.

I asked Brian what would be really fun and exciting that he had never done before. It took some searching but we finally came up with an exciting goal. He wanted to go for a whole year without a specific production goal and simply focus on really enjoying his interactions with his clients and new prospects. In addition, he wanted to trust and act on what his intuition told him to do on a day-to-day basis. What was exciting to him about these goals was the sense of freedom, creativity and the thrill of trusting his instincts to positively produce without a specific production goal. (Brian, of course, had to make a certain amount of money to maintain his lifestyle, so he did have a production goal indirectly. The key here is that he created a new focus that had more meaning for him.)

Brian had been in business for nine years at the time of this discussion. His tenth year was a record year by a 30% increase. In a review session at the end of his tenth year, Brian shared with me that he had never had so much fun working in his life and that the increase in his production without focusing on a specific production goal was "scary."

The Power of Visual Imaging

The concept of the visual image was mentioned in Chapter Nine, *The Mechanics of Maintaining a Positive Vision*. However, this concept is so important and powerful it deserves additional explanation. As you remember, a visual image is like a snapshot of what you want to achieve, using as many of your five senses as possible (seeing, hearing and all types of feelings, along with your sense of taste and smell). And, as you remember, you can easily put a series of visual images together to create an internal movie of what it would be like to achieve your specific goal. The key function of a visual image is to create a more accurate visual and experiential target for your analytical and intuitive minds to work on together. The more clearly defined the destination, the easier it is for your intuition to find a path to it. Or as Lou Tice says, "You have to make your goals more real on the inside than they are on the outside."

When you are creating visual images, ask yourself the following questions and then answer them in as much detail as possible:

When I imagine myself as having already achieved my goal, what do I see?

When I contemplate having already achieved my goal, what do I feel?

When I consider what it would be like to have already achieved my goal, what do I say to myself?

When I have achieved my goal, what do others say to me?

When I see and feel what it would be like to have already achieved my goal, what do others say about me?

The following is a visual image from my own life:

...It is early on a cold Friday morning in Denver. The sky is so blue and clear and the mountains are so white that it looks like a picture. I am on my way to Vail to ski for the day with friends. Before I leave I have to stop at the bank to get some cash and make a deposit.

I pull into the parking lot of my bank. I have a large envelope filled with many checks of varying amounts totalling thousands of dollars. I feel great! I had a very profitable work week and now it's time to relax and enjoy myself. I walk into the bank and up to the teller. She looks at me and says, "It looks like you are dressed to go skiing."

I say, "Yes, I thought I would get a few runs in today."

She replies, "It must be nice. I wish I was going skiing today."

(I smile, nod my head in agreement and *say to myself*, "It is nice. In fact it is really great and I deserve it.")

I say goodbye to the teller as she hands me my deposit slip. As I get ready to head for the mountains, I check to make sure my skis are secure in the ski racks. Then I jump in the car, turn on the tunes, and I'm off for a great day in the high country...

Have fun creating visual images (movies of your success) for as many of your goals as you can. Some people like to write out their visual images but that isn't required. Just get the projector running in your internal movie theater and make the events as real as you can.

Every day, set aside a few minutes of quiet time (while waiting for an appointment or killing time in a traffic jam) to enjoy the experience of reviewing visual images of what it would be like to have achieved your goals. Sometimes people will say, "This sounds great but I don't have any imagination." **The good news is that if you can worry, you have an imagination.** (If visualizing is not something you do easily, simply create the feeling of what it would be like to achieve your goals.)

The Key to Long-Term Goal Setting: "Make It Up"

One of the keys to successful goal setting is to know how to set long-term goals. The biggest pitfall for most people when it comes to setting this type of goal is that they are too reasonable. When you are setting a long-term goal, you should look far enough into the future that it feels as if you are "making it up." If you don't set your vision far enough ahead, your analytical and survival minds will limit your goals to merely repeating what you have already done plus a small *reasonable* increase in production. We are capable of far more than what our analytical mind can project with its limited perspective.

Imagine that you are ten years out into the future, or whatever it takes to disengage your analytical mind's desire to be reasonable. Then "make it up!" Envision what you would like your life to really be like! After you have completed your trip into the future, check with your intuition to determine if your new long-term goals somehow feel intuitively right and are aligned with your sense of purpose. Even if you have trouble imagining how you could possibly accomplish the long-term goals you've dreamed up (a good sign), your intuition can still tell you if you are headed in the right general direction.

Many things can and will happen in the next ten years to modify and change your long-term goals. This is fine. Expect it. The function of a long-term goal is primarily to provide you with a sense of general direction for now. Also, when your long-term goals feel intuitively right and are "on purpose," you will find they will lead you in the right general direction regardless of what they are. Furthermore, as you gain more knowledge and experience, you will also gain more definition on what you actually want to achieve. It is natural to make "adjustments" along the way.

For example, let's say you are navigating a sailboat toward an island on the horizon that is ten miles away and where you know there is a harbor. You sail toward the island until you get close enough to identify the entrance to the harbor and then you reset your course for the harbor mouth. As you get closer to the mouth of the harbor, you see the channel markers and again adjust your course for safe passage into the harbor channel.

When you started you couldn't see the channel markers. When you got close to the harbor mouth, you could. So is it true with long-term goals. When you get closer to achieving them you will want to make adjustments in order to reach your final destination.

One other very important item to consider. If you have done a good job at making your long-term goals as big as you can possibly imagine, I recommend that you don't share them with anyone unless you can trust them to understand the validity of this approach. Otherwise, they may think that you have "lost it" or that you have become a "legend in your own mind." My challenge to you is to have fun seeing how successful you can imagine yourself to be in terms of setting big goals that feel intuitively right. Remember that "adjustments" along the way are not only perfectly acceptable, but they keep you on course.

STEPS FOR SETTING LONG-TERM GOALS:

1. Look ahead ten years or whatever it takes to feel as if you have no restrictions whatsoever.
2. Let your imagination run wild. What are all the things you could possibly want to achieve?
3. Go back through your list and determine which goals feel intuitively right to you and have a sense of purpose.
4. Create detailed visual images for your long-term goals.
5. Create a "plan of action" by planning backwards from then until now.
6. Make appropriate adjustments along the way as you gain new information.

Regularly Update Your Goals

Be sure to regularly update your goals. You have heard the saying that there are two things you can count on in life: death and taxes. There is another item that needs to be added to the list: *change*. Things change daily in some way even though they may not be obvious at the time. You learn new things every day. You have new experiences. You learn more about yourself, and you learn more about other people, which also teaches you about yourself. You get answers today to questions that you asked yourself last week. Just a good night's sleep can dramatically change how you feel about things.

As these changes occur, your goals and visual images need to be updated to include the new information. What you wanted last month may have changed slightly now that you have new information. Priorities that were important last week may have changed with the latest developments in your life. The bottom line is that in order to give your intuition the most accurate target to shoot for, it is important to review and update your goals and visual images at least once a month to see how you are doing and if anything needs to be modified to reflect new information.

I now keep all my short-, medium- and long-term goals, visual images and descriptions of purpose on a word processor so I can easily make changes and updates. Some months the changes are minor; other months they can be considerable. In either case, I was amazed to find out how much clearer my goals and visions became once I got them organized and typed so they were easy to read. I found my word processor to be an ideal tool to update my goals and visual images when changes occur. My word processor eliminated the need to rewrite everything, which in the past looked like a lot of work and often didn't get done. I recommend using a simple word processing program on a computer to get your goal information organized, clearly stated and up to date. The more clearly your purpose, goals and visual images are defined, the faster your intuition will find the path to whatever your heart desires.

Affirming Your Goals

Affirmations are powerful and we use them in the conversations that we have with ourselves every day. I worked with an investment advisor named Kevin, who was constantly concerned about not having enough money to make ends meet, no matter how much money he earned. I asked Kevin to tell me what words he heard in his head when he thought about money.

He thought for a moment and said, "I'm always afraid that I will be short of money."

I ask him how many times a day he heard those words in his head and he said probably twenty times.

Then I asked him if he could see that **he was actually repeating an affirmation that said "I will be short of money" twenty times or more a day, and it was working!**

Kevin then changed the affirmation to "I now prosper and have a substantial profit from my work and creative endeavors. Thousands of dollars come to me now in many ways in an ever-increasing flow for the highest good of all concerned." As soon as he began to imagine himself as *financially successful* twenty times a day, he gradually noticed he had more and more money after he had met his obligations.

Take an inventory of the affirmations that you are saying to yourself, especially the negative ones, and replace them with positive messages. Positive affirmations are a highly effective tool to enhance your ability to achieve your goals.

The key elements of an effective affirmation are:

1. It must have personal meaning to you, something you want that feels intuitively right.

2. You must be able to clearly imagine what it would be like to have the affirmation be true.

3. You must have faith that the affirmation can and will become reality just like anything else you concentrate on in your life.

I have seen people work with as many as thirty affirmations at one time, but it is more powerful to pick a few and concentrate on them. An example of an affirmation that has been very successful for me is: "I am in perfect health, at my ideal weight and thrilled at the feeling of being physically fit, comfortable and full of energy."

Affirmations can be tricky at first because of the large discrepancy between where you are now and where you want to be. The analytical and survival sides of our mind are very skeptical of affirmations because they go against the current observable information about what is true about us right now.

I have found it helpful to have a conversation with the analytical and survival parts of my mind to acknowledge that they are correct. I agree with them that the affirmation I have created is not yet true and that I am creating a target for my intuitive mind so it can determine the best path to take to make the affirmation come true. I remind my analytical and survival parts that the affirmation will not become a reality without their help and that I need their full cooperation to make this project a success. Even though the analytical and survival minds like to be right about their information, they like to be part of a winning team effort even more. Acknowledging and working with the different parts of the mind goes a long way toward getting the *mental team* working together on making the changes you want to make.

More Balanced Often Means Less Analytical

If you are in the financial services industry, you have to deal with a massive amount of analytical information on a regular basis. Furthermore, the analytical information that you process much of the time is related to dealing with someone else's money, which they have entrusted to your care to protect and make grow for them. There is a strong underlying pressure to be very cautious and analytical in order to not make mistakes with other people's money. There is nothing wrong with being very analytical and making sure the course of action you have chosen is sound, but it can easily be overdone. Many people get so accustomed to being in the analytical mode they forget to come out of it. The biggest problem with being in the analytical mode too much of the time is that it is draining and a lot of hard work, and not much fun for most people.

How do you find ways to be less analytical in an analytical job and give yourself a break without jeopardizing the integrity of your work? Try the following activities that feel right to you:

• When you first meet a new prospect, relax, let the conversation wander a little and talk about some things that have meaning and feeling for both of you. Trust that if your prospective client has a problem that he wants you to help him solve, there will be plenty of time to get the business done, especially if he feels comfortable around you. The business aspect will get completed much sooner and with fewer stalls if you use this approach.

- If you keep track of a lot of numbers in your head, such as telephone contacts, appointments, closes, sales, etc., get into the habit of writing that information in your daytimer or something similar so you can forget about numbers for a month or more at a time and focus on enjoying your work with people. If you can arrange it, delegate the compiling of your sales activity numbers to someone else so you get a completed copy of your activity and sales results without ever having to add up a single number.

- Go to an initial interview with a prospective client without anything to write on and with no intention of taking notes during the interview. Simply say that you are just there to get to know him a little before you determine together what the next step might be. Then you can write or dictate some notes when you get back to the car if you want to.

- *Keep a record of the times you trusted your intuition, acted on its advice and then had something positive happen.* You will start to see a very important pattern. Positive results and other miracles usually follow trusting your intuition. (At least, they seem like miracles to the analytical mind. It's just a "day at the office" for your intuitive mind and its bigger perspective.)

Artwork for the Subconscious

Several years ago I made an interesting observation about the artwork that I had both at home and in my office. Without thinking much about it, I had chosen pieces that not only appealed to me artistically, but also represented things that I wanted to accomplish in my life. I had a beautifully rendered watercolor picture of my dad's old cabin in the mountains west of Colorado Springs in my living room. In my office, I had a breathtaking autumn shot of a freight train rolling through the bright yellow aspens along the Colorado River in Glenwood Canyon at sunset. One day I realized that I had the opportunity to buy a cabin that looked very similar to my dad's old cabin, and it was located in a spectacular mountain canyon near Glenwood Springs where I liked to go on weekends.

It occurred to me that I had looked at those pictures for several years and then, one day, along came a real-life combination of the two pictures put together. From that moment on, I decided to pay closer attention to the artwork I have around me in places where I spend a lot of time and make sure that it represents what I want to create in my life. Having attractive artwork around me that represents things I want and feel strongly about has a powerful positive impact on my ability to bring those things into reality.

Along the same line is the use of a customized "board," or large piece of poster board (usually used for picture matting; you can obtain many different colors at a framing or art store). "Boards" can be a great source of fun and creativity because there are no rules other than the ones you create. The main theme of your board is to find creative ways to represent your goals and your progress toward achieving them. The board can be of any color or size. The size will vary depending on where you want to display it. A popular spot for my clients is on the back of their office door so it is easy to see and becomes a constant visual reminder of their goals and their progress toward those goals every time the door is closed.

Now for the fun part. You can put anything you want on your board from cut-out magazine pictures to your own photographs, key phrases that inspire you or your own drawings. The possibilities are endless. One thing I usually recommend to my clients is that they pick a key number of cases, clients or volume of sales for their board. Whatever important number you would like to keep track of for the next month or next quarter will work fine. Once you have this number (let's say it's twenty-five new clients), go to the office supply or art store and buy some stickers. They come in a variety of sizes, colors and shapes.

Put twenty-five stickers on your board to represent the twenty-five new clients you want to obtain. The important thing is to then imagine that each sticker represents a person or a new client who already exists out there in the community and is waiting for you to make contact with them. They just don't know it yet! When you discover a new client, you simply write his name on a sticker.

Pete is a client in Colorado Springs who made a large board with 250 spaces for names. He looks at those 250 spaces every day to remind himself that those 250 people are already out there waiting to be contacted so they can become his clients. When he gets a new client he writes his name on the board wherever it feels right, so the names are scattered all over the board. His goal is to have the board filled with names by the end of the year.

Use your imagination. If you have support staff, get them involved and bring those dull production and sales activity numbers to life!

12. Overcoming Your Fear of Self-Promotion

A Prospecting Discovery

In the past I have had my share of "call reluctance," or fear of prospecting, or fear of self-promotion as we will call it in this discussion. And I can say that with a lot of frustration, determination, introspection and some courage, I have resolved the majority of my fears regarding self-promotion and have helped many others get rid of their fears as well.

There is a certain amount of fear or "stage fright" type fear that is natural in selling financial services. It comes from wanting to do a good job when you are trying something new or you are going after bigger clients with bigger problems to solve. The fear of self-promotion, however, is much bigger than the stage fright type of fear. The fear of self-promotion can absolutely stop you cold from doing critically important activities like picking up the telephone to make prospecting calls or to contact the people who you *should* be working with, just to name a couple of its many manifestations.

I will never forget the day I realized I could overcome my fear of self-promotion. I was on my way home from the office and decided to stop by one of my favorite parks in Denver--Bible Park. I do some of my best thinking walking around the park's perimeter, which is lined with majestic old cottonwoods. The rest of the park is wide open with many soccer fields and baseball diamonds. At that time of year, they were all filled with people playing in softball leagues. As I walked and watched people playing softball, it occurred to me that baseball is a lot like prospecting. The only real difference is that instead of making telephone calls to get appointments, you swing your bat at the ball being pitched to you. Your goal is to hit the ball in a way that allows you to get to first base or better.

Then I started to think about what it was like when I was at bat waiting for a pitch. I was excited. I wanted to do well and I wanted to get a hit. Equally important, I had forgotten about what happened the last time I was at bat.

As I was watching a batter take "strike two," I started to think about what it was like to strike out. I had struck out a few times and remembered there was some momentary disappointment as I listened to the ball hit the catcher's mitt and heard the umpire say, "Strike three! You're OUT!" But it wasn't a very big deal. Actually, shortly after I had struck out I was already imagining with great anticipation how well I was going to do the next time I was at bat. I had forgotten all about striking out within minutes, sometimes even seconds after the umpire yelled, "You're OUT!" Why was it so easy for me to totally ignore the failure of striking out when playing softball and actually be excited about getting up to bat again? When on the other hand, I would make one prospecting telephone call, have someone say "no," and instantly never want to make another prospecting call again as long as I lived? I was determined to find a way to have making my prospecting telephone calls be as easy and as fun as swinging the bat in a softball game.

Some Will and Some Won't

Let's examine some of the realities of self-promotion in the financial services field. First, you have to identify people who are interested in your services. Most often with financial services, you have to find *them*. There are several reasons for this. One reason is that financial advisors are a catalyst to get people to consider new ideas on how to maximize the return on their money and regulate the amount of risk they take in the face of changes in their personal or business situations. These changes can include changes in the tax laws, the economy and its impact on investments, and changes in the financial products available. Another reason you are likely to have to find your prospects, rather than let them find you, is that your prospective client has a fear of "being sold."

The fear of being sold has two basic parts. First, the prospective client feels that he doesn't know enough about the products available to make a wise decision. And second, the prospective client is fearful that an inadequate amount of time will be spent determining his needs and that he will end up with something less than the best possible solution to his problem.

In essence, your prospective client is looking for someone he can trust to put his interests first and come up with an idea or a solution to a problem that really fits his situation. The net result of these combined factors is that your prospective clients are going to work with you if you and what you are proposing feel intuitively right to them.

On the other hand, if you and what you are proposing don't feel intuitively right for any reason whatsoever, something will happen to slow down or stall the relationship-building process. No matter how good you are at your profession, you will never be able to comprehend all the feelings your prospective client may be experiencing. Most likely, your prospective client doesn't even understand all his feelings.

Therefore, there are always a few factors out of your control when you are attempting to get people to do the things they say they want to do. This brings us to a key premise that you must accept before you can be effective and comfortable at prospecting. In the process of attempting to establish relationships with prospective clients, realize that you can't please everybody. You and what you are proposing will feel intuitively right to some prospective clients but not to others, no matter how good you and your service are.

You may be thinking that the fact that some prospective clients will want to work with you and some won't is a fairly obvious premise, but stay with me on this line of reasoning a little longer and you will see where we get into trouble.

What Do You Say to Yourself After You Hear "NO"?

First, let's say that you have a goal for a certain amount of production and an adequate amount of time to prospect. Now, answer this question: Do you experience some hesitation, fear or resistance toward self-promotion? If your answer is "no," you have most likely resolved this issue and can skip this section. My congratulations to you. If your answer is "yes," however, the good news is that this is a logical problem to have and there is a logical solution.

Assuming that you are experiencing some hesitation, resistance to or fear of self-promotion at this time, think back to the last time (or any time) that a prospective client said "No" to you in any way. Now examine the following statements and check (√) any that sound familiar to you in the slightest way. These are examples of statements that you have likely made to *yourself* after a prospective client has said "No" to you in some way about what you were proposing.

AFTER A TELEPHONE CALL:

- "I want to talk to people who are interested in what I do. It's a waste of time to talk to people who aren't interested."

- "People should hear the logic of what I am offering and want to talk with me further."

- "People should be able to feel that I care about them and want to talk with me further."

- "People should be able to tell that I am skilled at what I do and want to talk with me further."

AFTER A SALES PRESENTATION:

- "People should be able to see that my proposal makes sense and want to buy it."

- "People should hear the logic of what I am proposing and want to go ahead with it."

- "People should be able to feel that they can trust me and go ahead with my recommendations."

- "People should see the value of the work I do and want to refer me to others."

- "People don't care about themselves or else they would see the value of my proposal."

What statements like these reflect is that a part of your brain doesn't agree with the prospecting reality that some people are going to want to work with you and some aren't, no matter what your skill level is or how much sense your proposal makes. Please note that I am not inferring that the above statements are false. There is truth in each statement. The key issue is that if you recognize any of the statements as a part of your prospecting reality, you are carrying around unrealistic expectations about sales and prospecting that are likely to cause some hesitation, resistance or fear of self-promotion.

The Internal Conspiracy to Avoid the Unknown

In sales, self-promotion and life in general, we don't get to know exactly how things are going to turn out ahead of time. We can make predictions based on past history, make educated guesses and take calculated risks. However, the only thing we can predict with certainty is that sometimes things will work out for us and sometimes they won't. There is always an unknown element about the future no matter how hard we try to get rid of it. This unknown element, combined with the interactions between the analytical, survival and intuitive minds, is a primary cause of the hesitation, resistance or fear of self-promotion.

Let's take a look at the three minds in action doing some self-promotional activity. No matter what your level of experience in the financial services business, the following sequence can happen at any time:

You have been working hard on several large cases for the past few months and have been maintaining your income in the meantime with smaller cases. Then a couple of the large cases come to fruition. Suddenly you're in great financial condition! You take a couple days off and smile a lot. You feel good about making things happen in your business. You figure you can give yourself a break from your self-promotional activities for the next few weeks because you have a little breathing room. But now several weeks have gone by. You notice that you haven't made any real efforts to get any new cases going. Oh sure, you have opened a few, but those are in the "lay down" category. You start to think about the "No's" and the hassle and the rejection involved in getting cases opened. Then you suddenly remember many other things that need to get done besides prospecting.

During the process of getting the large cases to close, the teamwork between the analytical, survival and intuitive minds was like clockwork. Everything seemed to flow together as you monitored your intuitive mind to determine what felt right for you. You negotiated with your survival mind to keep it from worrying and to get it to trust that something good would happen. You kept your analytical mind busy figuring out proposals and taking care of details. Then the big cases closed and you took a breather for several weeks. What happened during this period of time is that you lost touch with your sense of confidence and ability to self-promote or find new clients. You took a breather from the "unknown element" of self-promotion. You lost track of the fact that some people will want to work with you and some won't. You shifted to working full-time in activities that require preparation, follow-through and "filling in the blanks," engaging only in activities that involve minimal risk and few unknown elements.

A fascinating phenomenon occurs during a "no-risk" period. The analytical and survival minds team up against the intuitive mind and say, "Hey, this is great! We get to feel productive, get things done, feel professional, deposit some money in the bank (the result of previous risk) and feel good about ourselves. We don't have to risk getting beaten up in the land of the unknown elements. Let's see how long we can keep this 'no-risk' lifestyle going."

The intuitive mind has been out-voted 2-1 by the analytical and survival minds to maintain a "no-risk" lifestyle for as long as possible. Consequently, the intuitive mind is also on vacation because "what feels intuitively right" is temporarily unimportant in terms of risking any self-promotion, although it will give you a nudge once in a while during your "no-risk" period to let you know that something isn't right. This nudge to do some prospecting can easily be overruled by the noisy logic of the analytical and survival minds.

Even though they mean well, your analytical and survival minds have created the illusion that everything is fine and that in the process they have taken a dynamic, risk-taking, gutsy salesperson like yourself and turned you into an overcautious paper shuffler. Now how do you get out of this one?

Somehow you have to break up the conspiracy and get the intuitive mind back in the game. Without it you have lost your ability to see the big picture and have disconnected from your ability to know the best course of action to take. When you are disconnected from what feels intuitively right, it actually makes sense to hang out in the "no-risk" lifestyle that the analytical and survival minds have created.

The Accountant and the Adventurer

The path to getting back to successful self-promotion is entitled *The Accountant and the Adventurer*, named after the two mentalities or ways of thinking involved in the solution. The "no-risk" lifestyle is very much like the stereotypical mentality of an accountant. (In defense of accountants, they are complex human beings just like everyone else. My reference to the "accounting mentality" is only to create a frame of reference that you can easily relate to more than to describe a very demanding and necessary profession. By the way, my CPA has this information and uses it on a daily basis.) As you read through the two descriptions below, see if you can determine which way you think the majority of the time, especially if you are considering self-promotional activities.

The Accounting Mentality

1. Has a need to be right about his information and doesn't like to be challenged that his information is inaccurate or incomplete in any way. To have someone doubt or find fault with his information is close to a declaration of war.

2. Does not make mistakes. Wants to do things accurately and correctly the first time. Sees mistakes as not only unnecessary but humiliating as well.

3. Must have an answer for everything. If he doesn't know something he is supposed to know, he has failed to be the "all-knowing" expert.

4. Must make sense. There is no room for ambiguity or such unpredictable things as intuitive feelings.

5. Must maintain his composure at all times. Sees no need or value for such messy and unpredictable things as emotions.

6. Must follow the rules and fit in. Does not want to rock the boat or do anything that would risk disapproval or being disliked in any way.

7. Only deals with things that are predictable. The only risks he takes are on "sure things" that he knows will work out logically every time. Anything else is pure folly.

8. He must be totally prepared before he takes action. If he is not absolutely sure of the potential outcome, he is obviously not ready to proceed.

9. Wants to be in total control. If there are any elements in a situation that could be unpredictable, he should find another approach.

10. His feelings are hurt most when a prospect or client fails to recognize his superior talent, wisdom and knowledge and tells him "NO" in any way.

Furthermore, in the accounting mentality, it would be rude, presumptuous and unprofessional to do any of the following:

- Approach a prospective client to explain the value and benefits of the services being offered. (This should be obvious to the prospective client.)

- Ask a potential client to buy his recommendations. (The prospective client should understand the value of the advice and take his own initiative to buy.)

- Have to ask for referrals or to be introduced to others. (The client should want to share a good thing with his friends and associates, and take the initiative to make introductions.)

The Adventurer Mentality

1. Has an ability to continually see the bigger picture. Is not overly concerned with any one aspect, circumstance or event along the path to achieving the goal. Views the sales process, as well as life, as an ever-changing adventure rather than a predictable technical procedure. Knows, accepts and enjoys the reality that there is always an unknown element when working with people.

2. Has a tireless ability to maintain a positive vision no matter what happens, and keeps his eye on his long-term goal. Furthermore, with a positive vision and goals that feel intuitively right, he knows his visions will somehow become a reality with good for all concerned.

3. Trusts his ability to succeed and is not concerned with *how* so long as it is done with integrity and for the good of all concerned (the win-win approach).

4. Trusts the power of his intuition to creatively guide him along the most effective and efficient path to achieving his goal.

5. Has no fear of making mistakes since he sees mistakes as required events and lessons on the path to reaching his goals.

6. Has no fear of failure because he views failure as merely a negative judgment about how things have turned out thus far. His perspective says the only way to fail is to quit before it feels intuitively right to do so.

7. Does not need to know how things will turn out before taking action. He simply trusts that if he does what feels intuitively right with a positive vision, he will succeed in one of two ways. He will either get the result he wanted or get a lesson required to achieve the result. He knows in his heart and soul he can't lose.

8. Has fun meeting and getting to know new people. He enjoys being warm, friendly, spontaneous and "winging it" with people. He has a sense of humor and a sensitivity to what others are feeling.

9. Gives each call 100% of his creativity, skill and sensitivity. He treats each call as if it were a totally new experience, being ready to sense the subtle differences in people.

10. He does not care who buys and who doesn't. He is looking for the right people to work with based on the right "chemistry" rather than trying to "sell" a relationship to people who don't want one.

The Good News

Can you see how hard it would be to succeed with any sales or self-promotional activity while in the accounting mentality? There is nothing wrong with it. The accounting mentality is actually required to succeed. The problem comes when you allow the analytical and survival minds to operate without the intuitive mind. This creates a highly focused mentality that is too narrow to effectively deal with the unknown elements of self-promotion. The accounting mentality is required for things like adding a column of numbers or putting together the logical sequence of a presentation, but it is in trouble when you shift to dealing with the unpredictable nature of human beings and their feelings. Likewise, the accounting mentality is not effective at things like telephoning for appointments, interviewing to establish relationships, closing, asking to be introduced to others or any other self-promotional activity.

The good news is that the adventurer mentality includes the accounting mentality as well. It isn't a matter of being strictly one way or the other, although it may appear that way at first. If that were the case, the adventurer would be great at initiating new contacts but wouldn't have the competence to analyze the problem and determine a solution that the prospective client would buy. In other words, the adventurer mentality is the proper combination of all three minds: analytical, survival and intuitive. The adventurer is a balanced blend of the whole internal system. When the three minds are operating as a team, your internal system is in balance, and you will know what action feels intuitively right and be able to risk taking that course of action.

Mastering the adventurer mentality doesn't mean that you will never experience fear again. There is always the unknown element which can create some fear about the future. It does mean, however, that your fear won't stop you from taking the appropriate action, because there will be more of you committed to risking what feels intuitively right than there is committed to the "no-risk" lifestyle. Furthermore, when you risk taking action, your internal focus moves quickly away from fear to dealing with the matters at hand. An example of this would be when you are telephoning and you have some fear about making the call. When you actually dial the number and someone answers, your three minds switch their attention to what to say and how to say it. At this point your mental team has a more immediate problem than your fear, which fades into the background. Once your survival mind sees there's no danger, the fear subsides or disappears, at least for this one particular call.

You may be saying this all sounds great, but how do I get in the adventurer mentality and keep it?

The first step is to become aware of the cause of the problem as we have been doing. If you go back now to the section entitled "What Do You Say to Yourself After You Hear 'NO'?" you will see that these statements come from the "no-risk" lifestyle created by the accounting mentality. In order to escape its grasp, you have to become intimately familiar with the adventurer inside of you. How does the adventurer part of you think? What does he feel? What motivates him? Everyone has an adventurer inside ready for action!

Warming Up the Adventurer Mentality

Begin now to build the strength and presence of the adventurer inside of you. Search for any activity that feels adventurous to you. The following ideas and exercises provide some possibilities but by no means cover them all. If you come up with an interesting approach that works for you, I would love to hear about it. I, too, am always looking for new ways to keep the adventurer present in my life, especially after doing a few hours of highly analytical work.

• A very effective way I've found to get back in touch with the adventurer in me is to go watch adventurers in action. There are some great movies that consistently get me back in touch with the spirit of adventure. I get the most positive and lasting inspiration from movies that have a generally positive feeling to them and a happy ending. You will have to experiment to find movies that have the greatest impact on you. A few of my favorites are: *Top Gun*, both *Crocodile Dundee's*, *The Natural*, *E. T.*, *Firefox*, *Starman*, *Cocoon* and *The Abyss*. When you watch these movies, pay close attention to the positive feelings the adventurous hero stirs up in you. Really let the feelings in and savor them so you can take those same feelings back to the office.

- Create a visual image of yourself as a true adventurer in your current profession. What would you be like? How would you act? How would you dress? How would you talk? What would you talk about? How successful would you be? What would your day be like? What would your clients be like? What would you do after work? What would you do when you take a day off? Really get into it and mock it up! Dale Carnegie said it years ago and it is still true today: "Act as if it is true and it starts to become true." Part of being an adventurer is to risk letting some of that creativity out! Risk a little spontaneity! People are starving for some playfulness!

- Review your purpose and the visual images that you have created about it. Get into and daily relive the feeling of being at your best doing what you most love to do in your work.

- Feel what it is like to interact with people you admire and respect, and who genuinely appreciate you and what you are doing for them.

- Envision your favorite clients. What would it be like to set a goal for twenty more just like them, and not to waste your time with anyone else? Sure, you might have to talk to a lot of people but wouldn't it be worth the effort? For most salespeople, 80% of their business comes from 20% of their clients. Would you be willing to trust that there are plenty of prospective clients who *want* to work with you if you contact enough people? And would you be willing to stop spending time and energy with people who you don't feel some chemistry with fairly quickly? Remember, the adventurer is looking for people who "want to play" and "feel intuitively right," not people who need to be "sold" or "convinced."

- Look for examples in nature of the spirit of adventurers. I have an eagle that sits on my desk to remind me of the adventurer in the eagle. I saw a spectacular cable television program on eagles last year that gave me an important perspective. Eagles primarily eat fish if they are near water. They soar in circles high above the water watching for fish to come near the surface. Once they spot a target, they dive at incredible speed and at the last minute, just before they hit the water, they pull up out of the dive so that their talons drag open through the water and hopefully latch onto a big trout. Can you guess the number of dives it takes an eagle to catch a fish? Nine to ten! And do you think that the eagle feels he has failed and wants to quit if he misses on a dive? Of course not! 90% misses are part of a successful day's work for the eagle.

- What would it feel like if you knew you couldn't lose no matter what happened? Imagine yourself with the following characteristics: an alert sense of calm, the ability to intend a positive result with every person you meet, smiling and laughing often, having a playful sense about you, being confident, warm, friendly, inviting, unshakable, patient, easy-going, powerful yet sensitive, well-wishing, looking for those people you are thrilled to have as clients. When you imagine and feel these characteristics within yourself, you can't lose!

13. Connecting with the Right People

Trust Is a Must

One of the objectives many financial services salespeople have is upgrading their clientele. They want to work with people who have more money and bigger financial problems, which means the solutions cost more and they make bigger commissions.

It is generally assumed that before you upgrade your clientele, you have to know and understand how to solve the more sophisticated financial problems before you can get the wealthier prospective client's attention. It is true that at some point in the sales process, you are going to have to bone up on the alternatives available to solving the wealthier prospective client's problems, or you have to bring in someone who does know them. However, which comes first: having the knowledge or establishing the relationship? My contention is that if you are not effective at establishing a fairly deep level of trust and rapport in the first meeting, it doesn't matter how much you know.

In the financial services industry, the majority of the time people buy your solution to their problem because they like you (likability). They feel comfortable with you (rapport) and they feel they can trust you. If rapport and trust have to be present before your wealthier prospective client will take action on your recommendations, establishing that sense of trust and rapport is more important than any amount of information you could have access to. Furthermore, when someone trusts you, they expect you to come up with an answer that is the best possible solution to their problem and one that makes sense given all the circumstances. The ability to establish this sense of trust and rapport is the first step to upgrading your clientele.

What creates a sense of trust? First, it is an intuitive feeling, which means it involves millions of bits of information per second. When someone can trust you, it's because millions of pieces of information from his intuition take a look at you and you feel right to him. His intuition will consider the following items in the first five minutes of the initial meeting: how you look, how you are dressed, what it feels like to look you in the eye, what it feels like to stand near you, what it feels like to shake your hand, how relaxed or nervous you are, how easy it is to talk to you, your tone of voice, your speed of speech, the words you use, how well you listen, how confident you are, how easily you smile, how much personal warmth you generate, how sensitive you are to what he is feeling, how safe you feel. I could go on, but you get the idea. The intuition is an imposing "incongruence" detector for anyone who has his intuitive radar turned on and tuned-in.

Think about the most successful, balanced people you know. My bet is that they are very tuned-in to their sense of what feels intuitively right.

After your prospective client's intuition determines if you are worthy of additional time, he wants to know one key thing: "Can I trust this financial advisor to put my needs before his need to get paid? And can I trust him to come up with the best solution to my financial problem?" In other words, can your prospective client trust you to take the time to find the best possible solution to his problem even if it means that you make a little less money or have to wait a little longer to get paid? Maybe you don't even get paid this time around. If his intuitive feeling is "yes," you have a shot at his account so long as you maintain this level of trust.

Creating Rapport

What creates a sense of rapport? A sense of rapport, like a sense of trust, is a feeling that involves massive amounts of information being processed by the intuition. However, a sense of rapport and a sense of trust are different, too. The main distinguishing factor between them is represented by the following statement: You could be in "rapport" with a financial advisor at a cocktail party, but that doesn't necessarily mean that you would "trust" him with your financial future without additional information.

Rapport is a measure of how comfortable you are with another person based on having something in common. The more you have in common with your prospective client, the deeper the level of rapport. If you want to get a quick reading on how important rapport is to making sales, ask yourself how many sales you have made to people you did not feel a sense of rapport with.

The concept that being in rapport is having something in common with another person can have many manifestations. Think back to your last successful interview with a prospective client. When did the relationship move to a deeper level of rapport? It was when you discovered that you had something in common during your conversation. Maybe it was when you asked your prospective client, "Where are you from originally?" and he said, "Michigan."

You answered, "Oh really, so am I. Whereabouts in Michigan?"

He said, "Just north of Detroit," and you replied, "Is that right. I am from the Detroit area too! Small world, isn't it?" (Obviously you wouldn't say you were from the Detroit area if you weren't.)

Now this may sound like a small item, but it's how rapport works, one little piece at a time. When you have a bunch of those little things in common, you call those people friends. When you want to establish rapport, start hunting for things you have in common with the other person.

A lot of research has been done on establishing rapport in the past decade (see *Recommended Reading List*). The number of ways you can create rapport is mind-boggling. One of the key concepts is called "mirroring," which means you reflect back whatever the other person is doing, which then creates more things that you have in common.

An example of "mirroring" would be noticing that your prospective client is sitting with his legs crossed, so you sit with your legs crossed. You might think that this is getting a bit trivial, but don't knock it until you try it. Remember your prospective client's intuition is watching and sensing your every movement and will tune in to your efforts to be in rapport or create something in common with him.

Below is a list of some additional items you can match in order to establish rapport quickly in the first few minutes of an interview. All you have to do is pick one at a time. Trying to mirror or match more than one behavior could get in the way of effective communication.

Match body postures: If he sits back, you sit back.

Match body gestures: If he smiles, you smile.

Match movements: If he taps his fingers, tap your foot in a similar rhythm.

Match speed of speech: If he slows down, you slow down.

Match tone of voice: If his voice gets quieter, you speak more quietly.

Match breathing: Match the rhythm (movement) created by his breathing.

Once you have established a rapport with your prospective client, you don't need to consciously keep mirroring his behavior. You will both naturally maintain the rapport. A word of caution. Do you remember the saying "It's not nice to fool Mother Nature"? The same goes for trying to fool someone else's intuition. Don't mirror another person's behavior unless your intention is positive and it feels intuitively right to do so.

If you want to test to see if you are in rapport, simply take the lead by changing one of the above and see if your prospective client does something to follow you or mirror you. For example, a "test" would be to change the way you are sitting. If your prospective client makes *some* movement to mirror your movement (it doesn't have to be the exact same movement), you are in rapport.

Of course there are times when you want to be able to "break rapport." For example, when you want a meeting to end: If you have been sitting, simply stand. If you need to leave and you are standing, start moving toward the door. Also, looking at your watch is a good "rapport breaker." You can use this gesture to signal that you have to get on to something else.

Being Likable

Another important aspect of quickly building and maintaining a deep level of trust and rapport is being likable. An instant test to determine if this is an accurate statement is to ask yourself the following question: "How much time do you spend with people you don't like?" As little as possible, right? And when you are with people you don't like, you are probably trying to figure out a polite way to excuse yourself.

An easy way to create an inventory of how to be likable and what to avoid in order to stay out of the unlikable category is to trust your own experience. Think of three people you know and like and write down the things you like about them. Pay special attention to what they do that makes you feel good about yourself. Then take the other side and think of three people you don't like and determine what you don't like about what they do. This will give you a good starting list.

Make a list of the qualities that you currently have that you want to maintain, as well as a list of the qualities that you want to develop in yourself. It is important that you list only the positive qualities you want to keep rather than the negative ones you want to eliminate. If we focus on the negative, we get the negative. Don't try to *not* think about something, for then your mind dwells on that. For example, if I said, "Don't think of pink elephants," what happens? You have to think of pink elephants first before you can *not* think about them. Then it can be a hassle trying to get pink elephants out of your mind. So if you are telling yourself things like "Don't worry," or "Don't be nervous," you are living dangerously.

For any negative quality you are aware of in yourself, determine what the positive counterpart would be. For example, let's say that you don't want to interrupt people before they finish talking. The positive version would be to relax and enjoy your conversations with people and let them finish their thoughts before you speak. There is always a positive way to state everything. Become aware of it in your thinking.

Remember that your intuition has an unlimited capacity to process information, which means that there is no limit to how good you can get at being likable. The key is to review your list at least once a day and get a feeling for what it is like to have the qualities that you have described. You will find that your intuition will take the feelings of each quality and naturally blend them together into one feeling over time. You will also find that this "blended feeling" of all these positive qualities you want to maintain will feel very much like your sense of purpose.

Daily reviewing and feeling the qualities you want to have is one of the most powerful warm-ups I know for getting your day off to a great start. It also does wonders for your confidence and your ability to influence others when you can feel and know that you are a combination of many wonderful positive qualities.

Below is a list of qualities that I have found to be useful for developing strong positive feelings when reviewed on a daily basis. Because everyone has slightly different meanings and feelings attached to different words, you will want to make your own list. Look for those words that charge your most positive feelings. By no means is the following list complete. Whether you review five words or fifty, find the words and phrases that have the most meaning and feeling for you. Review them daily and you will charge out the front door in the morning! When you internalize them, you will come across as very likable to the people you interact with.

Think of what would it feel like to possess the following qualities as powerfully as you can imagine.

Words

confident, solution-oriented, tenaciously positive, powerful, integrated, balanced, decisive, practical, disciplined, effective, versatile, logical, fearless, articulate, fun-loving, highly productive, empathetic, intuitive, feeling, sensitive, forgiving, loving, caring, open, vulnerable, trusting, committed, inspiring, magical, kind-hearted, warm, gentle, patient, graceful, elegant, artful, emotionally mature, positive, impactful, healthy, financially independent, viable, profitable, peaceful.

Phrases

Possessing a "win-win" or "you and me" approach to interacting with others.

Possessing an ability to see the bigger perspective.

Being connected to a greater power.

Trusting and acting on what feels intuitively right with a passion.

Having faith and trust in your ability to choose the right goals and reach them.

Being confident in your ability to make the right choices on a daily basis.

Being driven to excel and express your true self in everything you do.

Quickly seeing the positive value in all events and circumstances.

Being energizing and empowering to be with.

Speaking from your heart.

Possessing a warm sense of humor.

Trusting your ability to consistently create positive results.

Possessing an alert sense of calm.

Seeing mistakes as a required part of success.

Being an unconquerable adventurer.

What would it feel like to have the above qualities all at once?

Who You Are Being

The level of rapport you establish during the first few seconds you are with your prospective client is crucial. The more you are being someone your prospective client can feel comfortable relating to, the quicker he is going to want to move to the next level in the relationship-building process. The most effective approach for being someone who other people can quickly relate to is to be the most positive version of yourself you can be. You have to trust that being the most positive version of yourself will be enough to meet and establish a relationship with the right people. When you are upgrading your clientele, think in terms of having more clients who feel like the "right people." The right people are the ones you most enjoy being with when you are feeling at your best. By taking this approach, you will naturally begin to find ways to prospect toward the kind of client you really want to have. Some of them are even going to have large financial problems for you to solve.

The other side of the coin is when you are being the best version of yourself and the relationship doesn't click fairly quickly. Politely excuse yourself and move on. If you feel good about who you are and you don't establish rapport with someone fairly quickly, trust that there is something major in the way of forming a close relationship. Yes, you could probably resolve whatever was "in the way" over time if you wanted to put in the effort. Or you could probably reach a level of rapport if you decided to contort yourself to fit what this other person is like.

The problem is that you very quickly get into the realm of doing things that don't feel intuitively right in order to make a sale. And, you remember what happens when you go against your intuition? The relationship will have some major failing or negative aspect to remind you that it didn't feel right in the first place. Why bother trying to work with people if you have to be someone other than your best self? If it isn't supposed to be, the relationship won't work no matter how rich and famous your prospective client happens to be.

I don't mean to imply that if you don't establish a sense of rapport and trust with someone fairly quickly that you should burn their prospect card in effigy. You may want to put that person's name on the back burner and see how you feel about him in six months. The "back burner" approach will be a little easier on your survival and analytical minds, which are often convinced that there are only a few prime prospects left in the world and that you should be more careful.

As a personal development coach, I get involved in every kind of counseling imaginable, including mending broken hearts. When I am dealing with someone who is convinced that there will never be anyone who could replace the love they have just lost, I say, "Well, John, it's clear to me that you have used up your quota of gorgeous, loving, talented women that God allowed you when you were born. You will just have to live out your life being alone and lonely. This is very sad, don't you agree?" This has never failed yet to get a smile from the broken-hearted. The same advice goes for losing (or eliminating) prime prospective clients from your inventory of potentials. There are always more where those came from.

14. Asking the Right Questions

Who Would You Rather Work With?

Let's say you walk into a computer store to purchase a computer and software which has many options to choose from based on what you want to produce with the system. In fact, there are so many options that you are at the mercy of the salesperson to help you figure out which ones to buy.

You are approached by the salesperson, who says hello and asks you if he can help you. You reply that you are thinking of buying a computer and want to find out what's available. Immediately you sense that your innocent question is going to turn into a nightmare, as the knowledgeable salesperson starts to tell you in very technical jargon all about the "T93 that just came out with the camoflux laser capacity and can accommodate 50,000 jigawatts input." Worse yet, the salesperson continues on, assuming that you understand every word he is saying.

Let's walk into a different computer store where you are greeted by a computer salesperson named Tom. The conversation goes like this:

Tom: "Hi, welcome, my name is Tom. How can I help you today?"
You: "Well, I was thinking about buying a computer and some software and I wanted to get some information on what was available."
Tom: "Okay, could I ask you a few questions to get a better idea of what you are trying to accomplish?"
You: "Sure, that would be great."
Tom: "Is this for business or personal use or both?"
You: "Well, probably a little of both."
Tom: "How familiar are you with computers?"

You: "Well, actually I have been avoiding them like the plague for the past ten years, but I'm afraid that I'm going to get left in the dust if I don't get one in my office and learn how to use it."

Tom: "So would it be safe to say you are a hesitant beginner?"

You: "Yes, I think that sums it up."

Tom: "That's no problem at all. Many of our most satisfied customers made their first purchases with us. We feel it's extremely important to help you determine how you are going to use the computer and make you knowledgeable enough so you can make the right decisions on what equipment and software to buy. That way, hopefully you will come back to us in the future. "

You: "Good, that sounds encouraging."

Tom: "Tell me more about the types of things you would like to be able to do with your computer."

You: "Well, I want to be able to. . ."

Which salesperson in the two examples are you the most comfortable with?

Why?

The basic difference between the two salespeople in the above example is that Tom cares about you and wants you to get what you really want so he gets another satisfied customer. He is taking the time to find out exactly who you are and what you want to accomplish. Furthermore, Tom is helping you figure out what you want because you have never had this conversation with anyone. You have avoided it for the past ten years. Doesn't it feel wonderful to be with someone who knows how to ask the right questions so you can determine what you really want? And I'll bet that if Tom kept asking you the right questions, you would end up buying from him even if it costs a little more. Why? Because Tom is demonstrating that he wants to make sure that you make the right decision. He wants satisfied customers. He wants repeat business and he wants to get your referrals.

Which of the two selling styles demonstrated feels right to you?

Double Your Sales

We have talked a lot about the fact that people have their own answers to the situations that they face in life and that those answers come from their intuition as what feels intuitively right. Because people don't always know what to do that feels intuitively right, they need someone to help them. This is where you can be of tremendous value to your clients. Help them determine the course of action that feels right to them, and they will be grateful and always happy to talk to you about your ideas in the future. So how do you help people determine what course of action is intuitively right to them? You ask them questions.

I was working with an investment advisor named Anne, who was very knowledgeable about her business. There was very little she didn't know about her specialty. She had a ton of energy and enthusiasm. No matter what you wanted to know about investing, she was ready to give you all the information you needed so you could make a good decision. The problem was, Anne was struggling with her business and no one could figure out why. She was especially frustrated with her slow progress because she had worked so hard to become an expert on so many aspects of her business.

Anne thought that people wanted information so they could make the right decision. The irony was that she was right. People did want information, but not just any information. What Anne failed to consider was that the information that caused people to buy wasn't necessarily based on what plan made the most sense or which deal was the best for them to buy. She was amazed at how many people didn't buy the recommendations that made total sense to her.

I asked Anne if she would be interested if I could show her a way to substantially increase her sales in less than a month. She said great, just tell her what she needed to do. I said I wasn't sure that she would like the answer, but she wanted to know anyway.

"I bet that you can double your sales in less than a month if you will learn to do one thing."

"What's that?" she asked suspiciously.

"Learn to ask the right questions."

She thought for a moment and commented, "You're probably right, but I don't know how to ask questions."

"Would you be willing to learn?"

She thought for a moment and then said she would. She confided that she really had nothing to lose since everything else she had tried hadn't worked enough of the time to please her.

Anne is like many people selling financial services who have learned to survive by their courage and the sheer determination to keep plugging away. It's a crime that so much talent and energy go to waste through ineffective approaches to selling. But when you learn something that works part of the time, it can be tough to scrap it for something that you have never experienced, no matter how good it is claimed to be.

For example, let's say that you have survived by giving people non-stop information, hoping that you will say the right thing. It would be very difficult for you to take the time to ask questions and find out exactly what people are really interested in and committed to before you ever present a solution. It's the timeless dilemma: "Oh sure, I would love to learn how to ask the questions that would double my sales, but I'm too busy trying to make a living. Give me a call in six months. Maybe by then things will have changed." Not very likely.

Anne put the same energy into learning to ask the right questions that she had into learning the investment business and turned out to be a star student. She more than doubled her sales in the month after we worked together.

Anne and I got together after she had closed a couple of very nice cases. She said she would have missed both cases for sure if she would have used her old approach of overwhelming people with information. At the end of our meeting, she thanked me with tears in her eyes and said, "Why did I work so hard for so long when it could have been so much easier?"

I consoled her with, "Had we gotten together before last month, you would probably not have been ready to give up your old approach and try something new. The timing has to be right and you were ready. Congratulations on being willing to risk and having it pay off."

Creating Emotional Leverage

You have undoubtedly heard the saying "Logic makes 'em nod their heads, emotion makes 'em buy."

What is referred to as "emotion" in a selling situation has several interpretations. We have discussed in a previous section that too much emotion can cloud a person's ability to make a good decision. So for this discussion, when we are talking about "emotion," I am referring to a strong feeling about trusting and taking action on what feels intuitively right.

So if "emotion makes 'em buy," how do you get people to experience that emotion? Being able to get to your prospective client's emotion and effectively use it to get him to take action on what feels right is what I call "emotional leverage."

There are several vital elements to getting and keeping emotional leverage. First, you have to CREATE A SAFE ENVIRONMENT for your prospective client to share his thoughts and feelings. By safe, I mean that there is no fear of being criticized or judged for the way he thinks and feels. You have to be willing to accept whatever he says and feels as absolutely okay with you, although you may find it necessary to gently re-educate your prospective client away from some misconceptions when the time is right. Your first mission, however, is to make whatever your prospective client thinks and feels the right answer for him. And you want to demonstrate this safe, nonjudgmental, accepting attitude toward your prospective client as early and as many times as possible in the initial interview.

The second vital element is to DRAW OUT your prospective client with questions. You want him to paint a verbal picture for both you and him of what he sees and feels that he wants. Remember, he may have never had the gift of having someone ask him the right questions to find out what really feels intuitively right to him. He is creating that with you. You also want him to have fun exploring and creating this together with you. To do this, you can ask questions like:

"Can you tell me a little more about that?"
"Can you give me a few more words on that so I have a better sense of what you mean?"
"Say more about that..."
"Tell me more about that..."
"Can you describe that a little more for me?"
"How would you know if you had that? What would it be like?"

You will also find that when your prospective client is answering your questions, he will tend to give you more informational answers at first and then move to more feeling-oriented answers as you encourage him. The conversation between You and your prospective client Dan might sound like this:

You: "Why would it be important for you to have a plan for your retirement?"

Dan: "Well, I think it is important to plan for the future."

You: "If you could realistically have whatever you wanted when you retired, what would that be like?"

Dan: "Gee, I'm not sure. I guess I've never really thought about it that much."

You: "I'll bet you've had some dreams about what you would want from time to time."

Dan: "Oh, now you're talking about dreams. Well, I guess I have a few of those."

You: "If you could have it any way you wanted it, what would it be like when you retire?"

Dan: "Well, I would want to have enough money to be comfortable and do the things I like to do."

You: "Sounds great. What kinds of things would you do?"

Dan: "Well, I would like to have the house paid for. I would like to travel some with my wife, and I like to do some fly-fishing once in a while. And I suppose if I had grandchildren, I would want to be able to afford to see them on occasion."

You: "How would that feel to be able to do those things?"

Dan: "It would feel pretty great."

You: "Is that an important feeling for you to have?"

Dan: "Yes, I guess you can say that would be pretty important."

You: "Can you feel that feeling right now, of having the house paid for, being able to do some traveling and some fly-fishing and seeing the grandchildren   on occasion? Can you feel what that would be like?"

Dan: "Yes, I can feel it."

You: "If you could come up with a word or two to describe that feeling, what would it be?"

Dan: "Well, let's see. How about peaceful and a sense of accomplishment."

You: "Sounds pretty wonderful to me. Are those important feelings for you to have Dan?"

Dan: "Yes, they are."

You: "If I could help you make sure that you have the financial resources to be able to feel that peaceful feeling and a sense of accomplishment, would that be important to you?"

Dan: "Yes, I guess it would, if you could help me do that."

You: "Dan, you work with me, I'll promise to do everything I know to do to help you get those things you want for your retirement. How does that sound?"

Dan: "Sounds good. What do we do now?"

Did Dan feel safe answering your questions and did you accept his answers, whatever they were?

Did you "draw out" Dan with your questions and get him to paint a picture of what he wanted?

Did you hear how Dan gave you more cautious informational answers first, and then moved to more feeling answers as you encouraged him to experience and feel?

Did Dan feel what was important to him? Did you feel what was important to Dan?

Do you think Dan appreciates the experience he has just been through? How many times in Dan's life do you suspect that someone has taken the time to help him determine what he really wanted?

Do you think what Dan wanted felt intuitively right to him? Would helping Dan get what he wants feel intuitively right to you?

How many times has someone else helped you determine what felt intuitively right to you? Did you appreciate it?

The real power in the conversation between you and Dan was the shared feelings. You shared the feeling of what felt intuitively right to Dan. There is no more powerful rapport and trust builder than to share the feeling of what is really important to someone. When you share an experience at this level, you are sharing millions of pieces of information and experience per second, and those are special moments. Remember that rapport is sharing something in common with another person. When you share at this level you have enough in common to be friends for life.

Sometimes your prospective client will give you all the information you want so fast that you can hardly write it down. Those are the easy ones. The more feeling-oriented people are, the quicker and easier it is for them to answer your feeling-oriented questions. They will also give you the emotional leverage you need to move to the next step in your sales process and eventually you will use this same information to close the deal. In essence, if you learn to get the emotional leverage with the tougher prospective client, you will be able to close many more of the cases you are currently missing. They need your help to figure out what they really want to do, and to determine what they feel strongly enough about that they will take action.

From what I have observed in coaching hundreds of financial services salespeople, the only way that your prospective client will buy your solution to his problem and have the business stay on the books is to help him determine what feels intuitively right. What feels right to him is what he will commit to and keep.

What's in This for You?

It takes extra effort to maintain your intuitive best. Therefore it's helpful to be aware of the situations that can fool you into thinking that you're doing all the right things, when in actuality you are not. This happens most often when you've been pushed into the analytical aspects of your work or when you've allowed a negative vision to creep into your awareness. When you've distanced yourself from your feeling side, you won't be as motivated to help your prospective client determine what feels intuitively right. Instead, you will unconsciously seek out the plan of action that makes analytical sense. The net result is that you will go through the motions of a successful interview, but you won't feel the things you need to feel in order to inspire your prospective clients to discover a solution that is exciting and empowering--the one they will buy.

Many people define "selling success" in terms of the bottom line. In other words, if you don't make a sale, you have failed or lost in some way. To the intuitive mind, the "misses" are a required part of success. "People not buying" is just as important as "people buying" to the intuition's bigger perspective. So if your criterion for a successful interview is whether or not you make a sale, rather than the thrill of being at your intuitive best in each interview regardless of what happens, you are headed for trouble. If you see "not making a sale" as a failure in some way, you will lose energy with each "No" and eventually run out of energy when you've heard too many "No's." This is commonly referred to as "burnout."

The following is a list of other personal rewards that can be obtained from "going the distance" to help your prospective clients determine what feels intuitively right.

• When you risk connecting with people on a feeling level and make it safe for them to determine what feels intuitively right, your clients will appreciate, admire and trust you more.

- When you stop trying to *get* people to do things and help them determine what they really *want*, your job will be a lot more fun. The struggle goes away.

- When you are being the most positive version of yourself, you attract the right people and other positive situations to you. This capacity to attract what you want can look like "luck" to the untrained eye, but is it really?

- When you *feel* a sense of professionalism, whatever that is for you, and allow yourself to be guided by your instincts, you develop a profound respect for yourself and who you are being. You become a positive force in life.

- When you are "out there"--being who you most enjoy being, feeling and trusting your instincts regardless of what others say or do--you get re-energized from every call or appointment no matter what the results.

- When you have given each interview all you've got, and done everything in your power to help your client make his own decision, you will feel good about yourself. You've done *your* job.

- When you trust yourself and risk acting on your intuition, you are instantly off the uninspired treadmill of "going through the motions." Your work takes on new meaning and things start to happen that make all the effort worthwhile. Working only for money grows old. Being paid to help people get what they really want, and then getting their smiles of gratitude and warm thanks, keeps a spring in your step.

- When you are in touch with the bigger perspective of your intuition, you can maintain a sense of humor about the events and circumstances of your life as well as a sense of pending prosperity and good fortune.

- When you trust your instincts to lead you to the fulfillment of your positive vision, you have the energy and state of mind to keep going, having faith that you will find the people you really want to work with.

- When you let go of the need to control every little step and instead believe in your intuition's ability to be in the right place at the right time, and say the right thing at the right time, life becomes a true adventure rather than a predictable, dull routine.

15. The Spiritual Connection

An Answer from Within

Being a personal development coach for the past nine years, I have had the privilege of helping many people work through the process of rediscovering what it feels like to trust themselves and reconnect with a true sense of who they are. I want to share an experience that I had one afternoon several years ago, because it clearly exemplifies one of the vital ingredients required to really trust yourself.

I was sitting in an office with a consultant friend, discussing the fact that I had some real potential that I was not tapping. I knew I could be more effective if only I could get myself more connected internally. It seemed that I was either very analytical or very intuitive and I could never seem to get the two working at the same time. The net result was that I knew I was headed in the right direction with people in helping them solve *their* problems, but I often couldn't articulate what *I* was feeling very clearly. This was very frustrating for me and was limiting my career.

I was very tired of being either in my intellect without any intuitive feeling, or being able to intuitively feel the right answer, but not being connected to my intellect so I could find the words to articulate the feeling.

Sitting with my friend, I asked myself, "Why am I either on one side of my brain or the other? What is preventing me from connecting internally so I can intuitively feel things and speak clearly about those feelings at the same time? I know that is what it's like when we are really at our best."

A few moments went by. My friend sat quietly, realizing that I was the only one who knew the answer for me and that I had to find it on my own. His job was to just "be there for me" so I could keep looking for my answer, because it was a big one. As I sat and stared out at the mountains, my mind went blank for a few seconds and then the answer came to me. I didn't hear it at first; I simply wrote the words out on a piece of paper on the desk. I didn't even know what the words were until I had finished writing them. The words were "Give it to God."

In seconds I felt a huge rush of emotion out of nowhere and I burst into tears of joy. The answer was so simple and I had been trying to figure it out for so long. It had never occurred to me that I couldn't connect myself internally without trusting in something bigger than just myself. In order to connect with all my personal power and ability, to reconnect with that sense of myself, I had to let go of trying to control every little thing and trust in something bigger that would allow me to use my intellect and intuition all at once. What a feeling! Life is so much easier when things are connected internally and so much easier when you believe in something bigger than just yourself.

Trust in Something Bigger Than Yourself

What does it mean to trust in something bigger than yourself? That is a question only you can answer. Everyone has the opportunity to choose what they are going to believe in and how they are going to interpret spiritual feelings. To connect with those spiritual feelings and keep them with you at all times is one of the most wonderful and powerful things you can do for yourself. My premise is that it's necessary to maintain a connection with "something bigger than yourself," whatever that is for you, in order to stay connected and balanced internally, and to ultimately be able to get at your true potential.

We talked about trusting and acting on "what feels intuitively right." Is it possible that in order to do this, you have to let go of the conscious control of monitoring every detail, step by step, and trust in something bigger than yourself to guide you to a positive result?

We talked about letting go of the negative evidence after you have maintained a negative vision for a period of time. Is it possible that when you let go of negative evidence and fear, you are trusting in something bigger than yourself?

When you think about your purpose in life, when you feel the power and strength that come from doing what you love to do and doing it well, do you ever sense that somehow your purpose is part of a bigger plan? Do you ever get the sense that there is somehow a bigger picture and maybe even a grand design or plan to all of life?

When you make the shift back to being an adventurer and once again risk dealing with the unknown elements of your self-promotion, do you ever get the sense that there is something much bigger than yourself watching out for your safety?

When you are connecting with the right people, when you feel that strong sense of rapport and trust, do you ever get the sense that those relationships are supposed to be?

When you are being yourself, being your best, creating a positive vision for the immediate future, trusting and acting on what feels intuitively right moment by moment, making wonderful things happen all around you, do you ever get the sense that there is something much bigger than yourself working its magic through you?

Yourself or YourSelf?

I heard a story once about a person who said, "There are two ways you can be yourself. One way is to 'be yourself' with the small 's' and the other way is to 'be yourSelf' with a capital 'S.'" The difference is simple and profound at the same time. Being yourSelf with a capital "S" is going through life trusting your sense of purpose, trusting and acting on what feels intuitively right and believing in something bigger than yourself. Being yourself with a small "s" is going through life merely trying to survive and taking the safest and surest course of "no risk" while you ignore who you really are and what feels intuitively right to you. Obviously, I am an advocate of being yourSelf and "Trusting YourSelf" with a capital "S," which is also how the title of this book is spelled.

16. The Art of "Staying on a Roll"

Trusting yourself and "staying on a roll" go hand in hand, because the best way to keep the roll going indefinitely, or get it back when it goes away, is to trust yourself. As a way to summarize, let's review some key concepts.

Key Concept Review

- *Define your sense of purpose* in a way that you can feel what deeply motivates you. When you are trying to determine what direction to go, take the path that gives you the same feeling as your sense of purpose. If you can't get that feeling with a particular course of action, it usually means that it isn't on the path to the goals you have set.

- *Formulate positive goals* that feel intuitively right and are aligned with your purpose. Learn to stretch your concept of what you are capable of accomplishing. Project yourself far enough out into the future to give you the sense of no limitations. Once you have specified future goals that are exciting to you and that feel right, create a game plan by looking backward over the events that would have to take place in order for you to get to your goal. In other words, go to a point in the future and plan backward instead of planning from today forward. If you simply plan from today forward, your analytical mind will tend to limit you to what you have been able to create thus far in your life.

- *Daily review who you really want to be*. Reconnect with your deepest sense of who you are when you are being your best, and don't walk out the door in the morning until you can feel it. Maintain an image or a feeling of the most positive version of who you are now and of who you can become.

- **Create visual images** for your most important goals. Construct clear images (snapshots or movies) of yourself as having already achieved your goals. Give your intuition a clearly defined target to shoot for by including as many of the five senses as possible.

- **Create a positive vision** for the immediate future, especially in the face of negative events and circumstances. Check in with yourself on a regular basis to determine whether your expectation for the immediate future is positive or negative. If it isn't positive, you are giving energy to a negative or unclear vision. Trust that for every positive action you take or positive intention you create, there will be a positive reaction returned to you in some way, although it may not be obvious or immediate.

Because our ability to shift our vision from a negative to a positive one is so simple and so powerful, it is often overlooked. We have accepted the illusion that changing the circumstances in our lives has to be more difficult than simply changing our vision or expectation of what we would like to have happen. Even when it *does* take more effort than just changing our vision or expectation, this is certainly the place to start.

- **Ask your intuition for what feels right**. Review the procedure for accessing your intuition. Learn to create an internally relaxed state of calm and ask your intuition questions. When you get an answer, trust that it is coming from your intuition's bigger perspective (the ability to process millions of bits of information per second), even if you can't fully understand it.

- **Take action.** So many times I hear people say they knew what felt right and they didn't act. What good does it do to have a positive goal, a positive vision, determine a course of action that feels intuitively right and then not take action? Without taking action on what feels right to you, you lose control and self-esteem at the same time. It is a good idea to examine what you could lose if your perception is off, but if you look at the down side and the risk still feels right, go for it!

- **Maintain a positive vision** by seeing the positive aspects of the events and circumstances that appear in your life. Trust that somehow, even though it may not be very obvious at the time, whatever is taking place in your life is somehow on the path to achieving your goals.

Remember that one of two things can happen when you: 1.) are in touch with your sense of purpose, 2.) have a positive goal, 3.) have a positive vision for the immediate future, and 4.) are acting on what feels intuitively right.

You will either get the result you wanted (or something better), or you will get a lesson required to ultimately achieve your goal. In three words, you can't lose!

• *Trust in something bigger than yourself.* Have faith that there is a purpose and design to the universe. Have faith that you will be given what you ask for. It is only a matter of time.

Trust that there is something bigger than you that you can connect with that is positive, loving, forgiving and a source of guidance.

From my observation, the properly balanced analytical-intuitive mind is so powerful and so fast, we *have to* believe in something bigger than ourselves in order to risk moving at the pace we are capable of at a subconscious level. Furthermore, it is difficult to experience a deep sense of purpose and truly feel inspired without feeling a sense of being a unique, important part of something much bigger than our individual reality.

You Will Be Tested

Regardless of how good you get at trusting yourself and keeping the roll going, you are going to be tested. It is a built-in condition of the physical reality that we live in that there is contrast, conflict and paradox. There has to be negative for positive to exist and vice versa. So since the negative elements of life are never going away, the real key is to master dealing with them in a way that minimizes their effect and maximizes our ability to achieve our goals in record time, without letting negativity stop us or get us down more than momentarily.

Because of the pressures of the business environment, it is very easy to lose our ability to see or feel the bigger perspective. People most consistently get into trouble when they lose the ability to maintain a connection with the bigger perspective that the intuition can monitor. Typically, people spend time doing the analytical tasks required in business and then they forget to shift back to a balanced approach of thinking *and* feeling. Or something happens to put them in a protective-defensive mode, and they forget to get out of that mode back to trusting their ability to have positive things happen with the effective use of their vision and intuition.

It is a safe bet that you are going to lose the edge of being on a roll from time to time. Your life will go along well, you will make the right things happen and stay in the flow, and then all of a sudden a crisis will appear and everything will come to a grinding halt. You may become fearful, doubtful or worried about the future. You may say to yourself that you really did it this time. How could you have been so insensitive and unaware of what was going on around you?

This is a normal occurrence and a normal reaction. It is also the critical moment that will determine the quality of your life, how happy you will be and how effective you are at achieving the goals you've chosen. At the moment things look as if they have fallen apart, you have to stop and take inventory of the essentials for staying on a roll. Determine what part of the formula you have dropped out and trust yourself to know what to do to get "on a roll" again.

Do you feel a sense of purpose? Do you have a positive goal? Are you maintaining a positive vision? Did you check in with your intuition and take action on its advice? Are you seeing the positive value of the events and circumstances as they lead you to achieving your goals? Are you in touch with what it feels like to be the most positive version of yourself? When things are not going well, it can be very difficult to remember these important questions. In other words, when you're surrounded by alligators, it may be hard to remember that your salvation is to maintain a positive vision and keep doing what feels intuitively right.

What Is It Like to Trust Yourself?

One of my favorite one-liners is from the movie *Raiders of the Lost Ark*. Indiana Jones, played by Harrison Ford, has travelled all over the world following clues that will hopefully get him a priceless artifact--the Lost Ark of the Covenant. In his search for the ark, Indiana miraculously escapes from one impossible situation after another. After many trials, he finally has possession of the priceless ark. Victory at last! Except almost in the same instant, a competitor archaeologist shows up with the German army to take the ark for himself.

As Indiana reluctantly gives up the ark to the Germans, one of his sidekicks asks, "What are you going to do now, Indy?" Jones replies in frustration, "I don't know, I'm just making this up as I go along!"

"Making it up as you go along." That's what it feels like to trust yourself and be on a roll.

It is creating a vision of how you want things to be and then maintaining that vision, no matter what happens to make it look as if you may not get where you want to go. Keep your positive vision intact, and check in with your intuition to determine what to do next.

Where most people fall down is when they say, "Hey, I didn't ask for this lesson."

We don't get to choose the lessons or the sequence in which they appear. Because we don't get to know the sequence of events and circumstances that will lead us to our goals ahead of time, we *have to* make it up as we go.

When I interview people who are "on a roll," they repeatedly say that the toughest part is to consistently relax and let things happen. You have to be able to maintain your vision and, at the same time, yield to the situations that arise, trusting they will lead you to your goal.

One client said that trusting yourself was like surfing. You paddle out far enough to get a good wave, then you wait for the wave that looks and feels right. Once you are up on your board, you don't have time to think, you just feel what there is to do and act. If you hesitate or doubt yourself for an instant, you usually get wet. And that is also how you learn to be a pro--taking a few spills and learning from your mistakes.

Trusting yourself is *not* about "getting it together," "looking good" or having everything you touch turn to gold. It *is* about listening inside for your calling, for what feels right moment by moment and then acting responsibly. Sometimes you are going to look like a genius and sometimes it may feel as if you've lost your mind. But what really counts is your willingness and ability to trust that if your intentions are positive, you can never really lose in the long run. You will reach your goals with integrity, even though it may look a bit unorthodox to the casual observer. Life is not a science, it is an *art*. You get to choose your goals, not the lessons along the way or how you will get to learn them.

Little Things Make a Big Difference

We all have the ability to profoundly impact our world on a daily basis. Great accomplishment does not come from one grand motion. It comes from the consistent efforts of people doing the little things the best they know how. Some of the little things are: setting a goal, believing in it and maintaining a positive vision when the going gets tough.

Make sure that the activities you involve yourself in have a sense of purpose, and regularly check in with your intuition to determine what feels right. Keep track of what it feels like to be part of something bigger. Believe that your positive intentions will be answered with positive results.

I am always amazed at people's responses when I ask them to list their accomplishments. A lot of times they will instantly go blank. Many people think that an accomplishment is some great deed, like being the best in their company or being recognized as a nationally-known expert in their speciality. These are great accomplishments for someone, but only one person can be the "best" or the "most." What about everyone else?

The thing you have to do, no matter what you are trying to achieve, is to trust yourself. Trust that being the person it feels right to be will create the life that has the most profound meaning for you. The things that move you--the things that give you the greatest sense of satisfaction and self-fulfillment--are the things that will bring you the greatest rewards.

We admire and revere the people in our world who achieve great things, but often the underlying little things go unrecognized. No one achieves any lasting measure of success at any endeavor without being true to themselves. They have to create a vision that feels intuitively right to them, trust their instincts to guide them to the realization of that vision and have the tenacity and singleness of purpose to not allow obstacles to turn them away from their dream.

Don't Lose Your Marbles

For several years now I have referred to my peak performance coaching program as *The Art of "Being On A Roll."* When I complete my work with a client, whether it be an individual or a group program, I give them a graduation gift which also serves as a diploma. I get out a bag of marbles and tell each person to pick the three marbles that feel intuitively right to them.

Why three marbles? There are several reasons:

- They can **SEE** them. This reminds them to maintain a positive vision for the immediate future and to keep an eye on their long-term goal no matter what happens.

- They can **FEEL** them. This reminds them to check in with their intuition for that course of action which feels intuitively right.

- They can **HEAR** them when they roll them around together, which reminds them to keep the things that they are telling themselves (affirmations) positive or in the "what's right" category.

- And finally, the marbles **ROLL,** which is a reminder that if they remember the first three things, one for each marble, they will be "on a roll" the majority of the time!

You would be surprised at the number of clients who tell me they have kept their marbles close by at all times. If it feels intuitively right, the next time you drive by your local hobby shop, stop and treat yourself to a bag of marbles and carry three with you. They are a fun reminder of how to trust yourself and stay on a roll.

We All Benefit

My mission in life is to share information that gives people a way to discover their greatest potential by being who they most love to be. I hope that as a result of reading this book and others like it you will join the growing number of people who are looking inside themselves for their direction in life.

Trusting yourSelf is what makes the greatest overall contribution to your life, the people you love, and ultimately to everyone else in the community. Learn to trust yourSelf, and we all benefit.

Appendices

Interview and Referral Tracks & Tips

The following information is a collection of sales "tracks," explanations and tips that have evolved from coaching hundreds of financial services salespeople to successfully increase their sales productivity *and* their sense of personal satisfaction from their work. If you are relatively new to selling financial services, this section will be a valuable resource to add to your training. If you are a seasoned professional, you will find this section an excellent review of the key elements for successful interviewing.

Tracking the Difference

There are several elements or steps that typically happen in a selling situation for the interaction to be considered successful. Often an outline of these steps is referred to as a "track." Like a train runs on a track, you can have a track for every part of the sales process which gives you a path to follow while you interact with your prospective client. You could have a telephone track, an initial interview track, a presentation track, a closing track, a referral track and so on. Having tracks to follow is very useful since it gives you a way to remember what you need to accomplish during each part of the sales process. A track also gives you the flexibility to be able to "get off the track" and not be at a loss for where to start up again when the conversation swings back to business.

Every financial services salesperson has some kind of track for any part of the sales process that he is doing with regularity. Even the salespeople who swear they don't have a track and say they do something different every time, actually do have a track. If you tape-recorded their interviews, they may use a different arrangement of words each time, but the basic elements of what they are doing from a psychological standpoint are predictably similar. So if you already are using a track consciously or unconsciously, doesn't it make sense to be using one that is the most comfortable and effective for you?

There are as many right ways to sell as there are people who sell. The same goes for developing sales tracks for the various aspects of the selling process. My intention in giving you the following track examples is to give you a general overview of the Question-Based Initial Interview Track, which is consistently used by the top producers in the financial services industry. Also, I have included some additional tips on organizing closing presentations and getting referrals. Use what I have written or modify it, or develop something that sounds totally different. The main thing is to get a feel for what you are trying to accomplish in each aspect of your selling process. Find an approach that fits your personality, that feels intuitively right and that gets the results you want the majority of the time. A little reflection and analysis of the effectiveness of your tracks can pay off in a big way.

The Question-Based Initial Interview Track that follows is designed to help your prospective clients determine what feels intuitively right. I originally learned this concept from Phil Kline, who was my life insurance sales manager in Lansing, Michigan. Phil is a master sales trainer and brilliant at helping people determine what feels intuitively right. I have made modifications to Phil's original track, but the basic concept remains the same. I thank Phil for permission to use the train diagram and many of his terms.

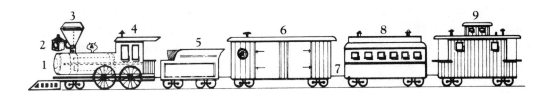

The Question-Based Initial Interview Track

1. WARM-UP: Toss some coal in the boiler by reviewing your vision of who you want to be in this interview. Get back in touch with your sense of purpose, create a positive vision for the immediate future and remember to ask your intuition for the best direction to go. Then trust and act on what feels intuitively right, whatever it is.

2. HEADLIGHT: Light the track by building some rapport with small talk, looking for things in common. **"Where are you from?" "How long have you been in the area?"**

3. "STACK THE DECK" WITH A GOOD INTRO: When the time feels right, give a brief overview of the general benefits of your service to clients. **"Let me give you a brief overview of what we do. Our primary mission is to help people maximize their return of before-tax dollars, and at the same time, minimize the risk."** (Then, generally and briefly describe a couple ways this can be accomplished.)

4. ENGINEER: The engineer takes control by getting permission to ask questions. **"So that I can talk more in terms of what might be of interest to you, would it be okay to ask you a few questions about your general situation?"**

5. TENDER: As the name implies, these are nonthreatening general questions designed to further establish rapport and begin to identify how much your prospective client knows, generally what he has done, and what he likes and dislikes. "Do you own your home?" "What other kinds of investments have your considered?" "What kind of investments do you like?" "Have you done any financial planning?" "What do you like about what you have done (or heard)?" " Is there anything you dislike about financial planning?"

6. BOX CAR: Start to box in and qualify what he has done and why. "This may be an obvious question, but everyone has different reasons for making the investments they make. Why did you pick that kind of investment?" Listen to the response. Then go for a deeper level and ask: "Why was that important to you?"

7. COUPLER: This is a way to shift the attention back to you and create some intrigue at the same time. "If I could help you accumulate money (or increase your net worth or become financially independent) and, at the same time, take some of the risk out of it, would that be of interest to you?" People usually respond, "Sure, that sounds good to me." This sets the stage for you to talk more about your service. You will find this an effective way to shift your prospective client from talking to listening.

8. DINER CAR (Menu of Benefits): Creating a "menu of benefits" is a highly effective way to focus your prospective client on the topics that you want to discuss with him. At a point in the interview where you feel the most comfortable, hand your prospective client a printed list of the items that you typically deal with and then ask him, "Would any of these be important to you?" or "Would any of these be of interest to you?" or "Do any of these look like they might be of interest to you?"

The following is a sample "menu of benefits" that you might hand your prospective client. This doesn't have to be a fancy piece of paper. This is a worksheet to write on. Some salespeople like to print the "menu of benefits" on their letterhead.

Check any of the following items that would be of interest to you:

☐ Utilize proven strategies to maximize return on investment and minimize risk.

☐ Tailor your (insurance, investment) plan to best suit your personal short- and long-term needs.

☐ Turn the odds of success in your favor and improve the consistency of your return on investment by diversification.

☐ Save time and avoid mistakes by utilizing the advice of specialists.

☐ Enjoy the "peace of mind" of knowing a well-conceived and safeguarded plan is in place.

☐ Work with advisors who understand and care about your personal objectives and motivations.

☐ Obtain the best protection for your specific liabilities with the life, health and disability insurance that will give you the most for your money.

You can actually create a "menu of benefits" right in your interview by asking your prospective client to summarize what has been important in your discussion thus far. **"John, could you summarize for me what you think are the one or two things that we have talked about today that would be of the most potential interest to you?"**

9. CABOOSE: This is a series of questions designed to isolate the main interests of your prospective client and to identify his strongest motivations on a feeling level. It is very helpful to jot down the answers to these questions as you go through them, summarizing in your prospective client's own words, since you will want to be able to repeat them back to him. There is an example of what the "Caboose" section of the track would sound like in the conversation between "You and Dan" in the section called *Creating Emotional Leverage* on page 115.

A.{PICK MOST IMPORTANT} **"John, of the items that you circled on the sheet, which one would be the most important to you?"**

B. {WHY IMPORTANT?} **"You know John, many people say the same thing. I am curious. Why is that important to you?"** or **"This may sound like an obvious question but everyone gives me a different answer...Why is it important to you to have** (his answer from question A)?"

C.{FUTURIZE} **"John, let's say you were able to have** (his answer from question A) **and** (his answer from question B)." **"What would that be like?"** or **"What would that look like?"** or **"Could you describe that for me a little so I have a better idea of exactly what you would want?"**

D. {HOW'S IT FEEL?} "If you had (his answer from question A), (his answer from question B) and (his answer from question C), how would that feel to you?"

or "If you had all those things, how would that feel?"

E. {CAN YOU FEEL IT NOW?} "Can you feel that feeling right now of what that would be like to have those things you really want?"

F. {IS THAT IMPORTANT?} "Is that important to you, John, to have that feeling?"

G. {SUMMARY CLOSE} "Okay, John; you work with me (us), you will have
(his answer from question A),
(his answer from question B),
(his answer from question C), and most important you'll have that feeling of
(his answer from question D).
Is that what you want?"

{PROMISE CLOSE} "Okay, John; you work with me (us), I promise to do everything I know how to do to help you get those things you want. How does that sound to you?"

H. {SET TIME FOR FACTFINDER} "In order for me to do my job, I need to schedule a time to get some additional information from you..."

NOTE: As I am sure you have experienced, you never know exactly what is going to happen in an interview. Sometimes you can follow your track very closely, and other times you will wander all over the place. The beauty of having a track is that you can wander and still cover the critical steps to get a commitment from a prospective client to move to the next step in the process.

My Favorite Interview Questions

The following is a list of some of my favorite interview questions:

Drawing out a description:
"Can you tell me a little more about that?"
"Can you give me a few more words on that so I have a better sense of what you mean?"

"Say more about that…"
"Tell me more about that…"
"Can you describe that a little more for me?"
"How would you know if you had that? What would it be like?"

Getting people to see the value of what you are saying:
"What are you most appreciating about what I've been saying?"
"What value do you see in what I've presented?"
"What do you find useful about what I've been saying?"

Helping people discover what is important to them:
"Is this important for you to have?"
"Is this something that would be nice, or is it something you are committed to having?"
"How would it feel to have this (that)?"
"Is that an important feeling for you to have?"

Getting people to go to deeper levels of feeling:
"This may sound like an obvious question, but why is that important to you?"
"Many people say that is important to them. Why is that important to you?"
Whatever their answer you ask: "And why is *that* important to you?"
(Repeat the last question after informational answers until you get a feeling-oriented response.)

Getting people to look for what feels intuitively right:
"If you could do anything you wanted, what would feel intuitively right?"
"What feels intuitively right to you?"
"What seems to really fit for you?"
"What can you really get excited about?"
"Which approach is the most energizing?"
"Which approach gives you the greatest thrill?"
"If nothing mattered, nobody cared and money wasn't an issue, what would you do?"

Responses to "I want to think it over…":
"I don't need a decision from you now, but how does what we have talked about feel to you?"
"What needs to happen for it to feel right enough to go ahead?"
"What do we need to change to make it feel right?"
"I'm not so concerned about what your decision is. I just want you to make a decision that feels right. What feels right at this point?"

"When do you want to make that decision by?"
"What do you want me to do?"
"What's next for us?"

Interviewing Tips

- Approach each interview newly with positive anticipation and the enthusiasm and energy level of your best interview. Set a goal to make each new interview your best ever.

- Be calm, relaxed, peaceful and visualize a positive result for the meeting. See yourself and your prospective client enjoying each other's company, and let your intuition guide you through your track while you trust and act on what feels intuitively right.

- Help your prospective client discover what he really wants (what feels intuitively right to him) and he will find the energy, drive and commitment to take action now.

- Create a safe (nonjudgmental) environment in which your prospective client can freely share his thoughts and feelings without fear of being negatively judged in any way. In other words, encourage your prospective client to talk by asking him sincere questions and then demonstrating that it is safe for him to share anything with you by accepting whatever he says.

- "Draw out" your prospective client by getting him to describe in detail what he wants, how he feels and why he feels that way. To have your prospective client feel safe enough around you to be able to share what he truly feels, and at the same time know he will be accepted by you, is a powerful experience that people can't get enough of and will come back for more.

- Focus on what is right or of value about your prospective client and whatever actions he may have taken thus far. Bringing out what is right about people and validating the choices they have made builds the energy required for them to want to make more decisions with you. Dealing solely with what is wrong or pointing out mistakes drains energy and creates a fear of making more decisions that could result in more mistakes.

- Help your prospective client experience what it feels like to have made some good decisions along the way. Help him feel good about himself. Use your observation and intuition to find something that you admire or respect about him and tell him about it sincerely. Tell him what you like about what he has done. Tell him what you like about what he hasn't done. Whatever he has done, find a way to compliment him. If the compliment is sincere, you will always be a special person to him.

- Minimize technical explanations and keep it simple and of specific interest to your prospective client (KISS). Most people don't really care how it works in detail. They want to know if it will effectively solve their problem and how it will feel to own it. If you find yourself spending a lot of time in technical explanations, "check in" regularly with people and ask them if what you are saying makes sense and ask them how they are feeling about the explanation. If you give people a chance to change the subject, you may find that they don't really want to talk about the technical aspects of the proposal. But they do want to talk about how they feel on a nontechnical level.

- Make it easy for your prospective client to laugh and have fun. Get the seriousness out of your interview. Business is serious enough already. You want him to have a great time with you and get some important things accomplished at the same time. That is how people really want to do business anyway. You want your prospective clients to associate feeling good, having more energy and having fun with being around you!

You also want your prospective client to work with you because it feels intuitively right to both of you and makes sense at the same time. If he feels good being around you, there is a connection on a personal level. That connection is a shared feeling of rapport and trust. Being able to establish this level of rapport and trust is the foundation for building your clientele and your career.

Closing Presentation Format

The following is a format for a closing presentation using the information obtained from the Question-Based Initial Interview Track. The KISS rule applies here. Keep it simple and specific to your prospective client's interests. Create your own checklist of the key issues you want to address in your presentations and the order in which you want to present them.

PRIMARY INTEREST: What are the main things your prospective client is trying to accomplish?

WHY IMPORTANT: Why is it important to him? What does it accomplish materially and emotionally? What are his strongest motivations on a feeling level?

EXPECTED OF ME: What does he expect of me and why is that important to him materially and emotionally?

EXPLANATION: Whatever you are going to propose--insurance, investments, etc.--teach him enough so that he understands the basics of the solution you are going to be presenting. Keep it simple and specific to his interests (KISS).

STRONG POINTS: What has he done right? Compliment him on what he has accomplished so far, the foresight that he has shown, the validity of his plans, his concern for the future and whatever else you feel appropriate.

MAJOR PROBLEM: What is the major obstacle in the way of accomplishing his goals for the immediate future that he wants to address? Get agreement that this is the main problem and that he is committed to doing something about it. *Don't offer a solution until you have an agreement on what the problem is and a commitment to solve the problem in the most effective way.*

SOLUTION: Your solution to the major problem, including presentation material: proposals, computer printouts, ledgers, etc.

WHY NOW: Outline the reasons to do it now and have them ready to go!

OTHER CONSIDERATIONS: What other considerations outside your immediate area of expertise do you see that may need some attention? You want to be seen as an advisor who has a perspective on the big picture and who is concerned for the overall success of your prospective client's program.

OBJECTIONS: Anticipate why you think or feel he would stall or object to your proposal and/or why he would object to getting started now, and be prepared. Obviously, he has to do what feels intuitively right to him. However, you want to do everything you can to get him to do what he said he wanted to do and take action toward that aim.

NEXT STEP: What is the next step? Get agreement and commitment to whatever is to be done next.

The Psychology of Getting Referrals

There are many ways to prospect, but consistently one of the most effective for many financial services salespeople is to get referrals from their clients to the people they know. Asking for referrals can be challenging for all the same reasons that selling is challenging. You have to keep track of the fact that you have a quality service to offer. You have to remember that you personally have a lot to offer people because of your quality approach to doing business. And you have to be able to maintain this positive vision about yourself regardless of how other people react to you. Some people are going to help you and some are not, regardless of what you do.

In general, the trends in marketing professional services are becoming more and more personal. With our increasing dependence on computers and the growing reality that your account number is often more important than your name, people more than ever want to feel some connection to the people they work with, especially financial advisors. Being introduced to a service (your service) that puts the needs of the individual first, by a friend or an acquaintance, is a very natural and accepted way to market.

Furthermore, if you are going to be in the relationship business, isn't it only natural to let the relationships you have promote you? You have worked hard to develop and maintain your client relationships and they appreciate your efforts to be available to them. In many cases, "being available" is a key motivating factor for why a prospective client will choose one advisor over another. Your clients appreciate having someone they feel safe talking to about their personal matters. Your clients also want you to do well and are very often willing to help.

Why do clients need to be encouraged to give you referrals? Think about what criteria you would have for giving a financial advisor names of people to call.

Let's assume for a moment that you have worked with Frank, the financial advisor, and that you liked the work he did. Would you offer the names of your friends right there on the spot unsolicited? Probably not. You aren't sure that Frank even wants names. It might not even occur to you to offer names unless you had some knowledge of the sales process. You may feel that your friends have their own advisors who they are happy with, and that you don't want to involve yourself in such a personal issue. If you did suspect that Frank would like some names, wouldn't you feel better about Frank's confidence level if he asked you for them? And even if Frank did ask you for names, you would have to consider how you would look to your friends by referring Frank. Would people think more or less of you for referring Frank? By no means is this a complete study on the psychological implications of asking for referrals. You get the idea by now that this can be an incredibly complex issue for both you and your client if it isn't handled properly.

Tips on Getting More Referrals

The following suggestions will help you simplify your approach to asking for referrals and substantially increase the likelihood of having the process be a more positive and rewarding experience.

- Check your vision about your ability to get referrals from clients. Is it a positive expectation of success or a fear of potential rejection or failure? You have to be willing to let go of any negative evidence that you have collected in the past about your ability to get referrals. Push the erase button on all the negative tapes in your mind. Pretend that you just woke up on planet Earth today and have no idea where you came from and no past. Now create a visual image of yourself asking a client for referrals and have him smiling and saying that he would be happy to help you. If you feel resistance to creating this vision or think it won't work, you haven't let go of the old negative evidence yet.

- Remember, asking for referrals is a mini "sale" and requires an "adventurer" mentality. (Review the qualities of the adventurer mentality if necessary to capture this feeling.) Basically, you give it your best shot and don't worry about whether people give you names or not. Some will and some won't. Your job is to explain the benefits you can provide for your potential client's friends, let your clients do whatever they do, accept whatever makes sense to them and then forget about it. As soon as you think you should be getting referrals from everyone every time, you are heading for disappointment because selling doesn't work that way and never will.

NOTE: A common illusion among people going through the "asking for referrals" process is that when you ask for referrals, there is a strong possibility that your client will immediately go into a rage, cancel his business with you, throw you out of his office and tell you he never wants to see you again. The good news is that your imagination is working; the bad news is that this type of vision is going to make it next to impossible to start asking. Take some time to interview some of the more experienced people in your profession and ask them how many times they have lost business or clients because they asked for referrals. You will find the responses very consistent.

- The following is crucial: Think in terms of "getting introduced" rather than "getting referred." Getting referred implies an endorsement to a lot of people. The problem with an endorsement is that your client will tend to think in terms of trying to figure out who he knows who needs what he just bought. Financial matters are very personal, and it is unlikely that your client really knows very much about anyone else's financial situation. Even if he is familiar with a friend's finances, he may be uncomfortable referring you because it could make him look as if he is sharing confidential information with outsiders. You may want to let your client know that you are not necessarily looking for people who need the same products or services that he just purchased. Everyone is different and has different needs. You simply want to be introduced to people your client knows in order to have a brief and general discussion to see if there is enough chemistry (rapport) and potential interest to proceed.

    In other words, I don't want my client to be thinking, "Who do I know who needs life insurance?" or "Who do I know who needs tax shelters?" (Of course, there are exceptions.) I *do* want my client to be thinking, "Who do I know who I could introduce Frank to? If there is the right chemistry and interest for them to do business, great. If they decide not to work together for whatever reason, that is up to them. I am simply introducing someone to my friend who has been of great help to me. I am telling him about a good thing."

    Asking for referrals is simply a natural networking process at work. "Would you be willing to let me send some information to the people you know if you liked my program? My guess is that you would be willing to help me." Getting introduced to your client's friends should be that uncomplicated.

- Make it safe for your client to say "no" by giving him a way out on the front end. When you bring up the discussion of being introduced, say that you would like to ask for your client's help, but only if he feels comfortable with your process. If he doesn't feel comfortable in any way with your introduction process, you don't want him to feel an obligation to get involved. An interesting phenomenon occurs when you give your clients a way out: they say "yes" more often. Besides, you don't want your clients to introduce you if they are not comfortable doing so. But you do want to do everything possible to make it comfortable, easy, convenient and inviting for them to promote a good thing: *you.*

- Make a commitment to a certain number of introductions (referrals) each month. Develop and practice a "referral track." Create a positive visual image of yourself successfully obtaining referrals on a regular basis. Review that vision daily and begin to risk giving clients your "referral talk" and your intuition will do the rest. The secret is in making the commitment to ask for referrals or ask to be introduced so you get some practice. You can't learn to be effective at getting referrals unless you ask enough times to let your intuition get a feel for it. Trying to learn to ask for referrals by worrying about what could happen and not taking action is like trying to learn to swim on the beach. At some point, you have to wade out into the water and find out what it feels like and what works for you in order to swim. You are not going to be an expert swimmer the first time in the water, but every time you go in the water it gets a little more comfortable. Once you're comfortable and proficient in the water, it is often hard to remember what the big deal was when you were first learning how to swim.

The first step toward being an expert is to risk being a beginner. This *is* the shortcut.

Sample Language for Getting Introduced

Take the essence of the following language and make it your own. Reword it, rearrange it, but do have a track that you are comfortable with and that you have role-played with friendly, nonjudgmental supporters. Put your language on a cassette tape and listen to it in the car until it becomes a part of you. Asking for referrals or asking to be introduced should be as natural as asking a good friend for a favor.

(GET POSITIVE AFFIRMATION of the job you did.) "John, how do you feel about the work I have done for you?" "What did you like in particular?" or "Specifically, what did you like?"

(BE PATIENT here. Give him time to come up with an answer that feels right to him. The reason for doing this is to refocus your client back on the fact that you did a good job and that he is pleased. When people feel good about something, they want to tell their friends about it.)

"John, I have a favor to ask," or "I would like to ask you for your help. And I don't want you to help me unless it feels right to you." (Pause, breathe.)

"The majority of my business comes from being informally introduced by my clients. And I mean informally introduced in the truest sense."

"What I do is send people this letter (show letter) that generally mentions what I do and more important, at the bottom of the letter it says that you know me. This isn't an endorsement of any specific product or service. The business that you and I did together is strictly confidential. What this letter says is simply that you know me, that I am someone worth meeting, and that I work in the financial services area."

"I find that people will rarely call you to ask about me. However, the reason I will get in to see them is because your name is at the bottom of this letter as a reference. For most people, if there is someone's name at the bottom of the page that they know, they will meet with me for a few minutes as a courtesy to you and then make their own decision if they want to take it any further."

"If it turns out that your friend and I get along and he or she wants to do business with me, great. If we don't find any reason to work together at that point, we each have another person in our network and you never know when you might be able to help each other out. I find the more people I know, the better I can serve my clients."

"Would you be willing to informally introduce me to people on this basis?"

"Who do you know who's doing well?"

When you are talking about (qualifying) the people your client knows, ask him what he likes about him or her. This then allows you to open your telephone conversation with a compliment:

(Warmly and sincerely) "I was talking to (your client's name) recently and he had some very complimentary (good) things to say about you." (Pause, let him feel it.) "And that's why I sent you the letter. I wanted to have a chance to meet you and talk for just a few minutes, and I was wondering if you could fit me in your schedule for about fifteen minutes some time in the next couple weeks?"

Sample Introduction Letter

The following letter is a modified version of an idea that I got from Hugh Thompson in 1975. Hugh Thompson is one of the all-time greats in the life insurance business. When I met him, he was traveling the country sharing some of his most successful techniques. I found this letter to be extremely effective both for me and for hundreds of my financial services clients. What the body of the letter says is of secondary importance to the fact that your client's name is underlined or in bold letters at the bottom. That is the first thing that your referred prospect sees and that is also why he will read and remember the letter when you call.

(Your Letterhead)

Date

Person U. Wannameet
241 Prospect Court
Anytown, US 54321

Dear Person:

Within the next few days, I will be contacting you to ask your permission to meet with you at your convenience. I have no reason to believe you are presently interested in equity investments or insurance planning, but you have been described to me as a person who is interested in constructive ideas.

My ideas involve ways to maximize your "before-tax" income. I assure you that I will be brief and that subsequent meetings will be arranged at your request. I will not attempt to sell you any products during this interview. I simply want to meet you and share some information that has been very valuable to many people like yourself. I hope that we can get together on this basis.

Sincerely,

Will U. Followup

WUF/bhs

P.S. Prior to my calling, you may want to refer to (*Introducer's Name*) regarding me and the type of service I offer.

Closing Thoughts...

For years I thought that once you finished reading a book, there was no reason to pick it back up again. However, I have found it very valuable to reread parts of several books from time to time. This is partly to see how much of the material I have internalized, and I am always fascinated to notice that as I grow and change, so does the information I get from my favorite books.

One of my motivations for writing this book was to give people a resource that they could review to "get the juices flowing" again. I now have lots of feedback that this book is being read and reread regularly to get people out of the "stuck" position and back "on a roll." So if your intuitive instincts tell you to review this book from time to time, you know what to do.

Please drop me a note to let me know how this book has been helpful to you. It doesn't have to be anything fancy. Hearing from you is a validation for both of us; for you when you put your experience down in words, for me when I get to share your experience. I'm sure you'll agree that knowing we made a difference in someone's life is what makes it all worthwhile.

Thanks for the opportunity to share an important part of my life with you.

Good luck to you!

Recommended Reading List

The following are my favorite books under each subject heading. They are by no means the only good books on these subjects. I recommend them here because I have had consistent success in using these books with my clients. I have provided a brief comment about each book to help you determine what additional reading might be best suited for you.

COMMUNICATION & RAPPORT

Influencing With Integrity: Management Skills for Communication and Negotiation by Genie Z. Laborde, Syntony Publishing, $12.95. (Easy reading, well-organized book on advanced communication and sales techniques from a "win-win" point of view.)

You Are The Message: Secrets of the Master Communicators by Roger Ailes, Dow Jones Irwin, $19.95. (The personal coach to some of the most powerful people in America shares his secrets on persuading, influencing and entertaining others.)

Unlimited Power: The Way to Peak Personal Achievement by Anthony Robbins, Fawcett Columbine, $9.95. (An exhaustive study on the principles and applications of "modeling" excellence based on Neuro Linguistic Programming - NLP. Read the first five chapters to get the message, then pick and choose.)

GOAL SETTING

The Path of Least Resistance: Principles For Creating What You Want To Create by Robert Fritz, DMA, Inc., $14.95. (Profound and practical. Well-defined and well-organized principles for creating what you want to create.)

INTUITION

Living In The Light: A Guide to Personal and Planetary Transformation by Shakti Gawain, Whatever Publishing, $8.95. (A brilliant book on intuition, a feminine point of view written in very practical, clear language. This one changes many lives. Start with the chapters on intuition and you have the message. Read on from there if it "feels intuitively right.")

MARKETING

Money Making Marketing: Finding The People Who Need What You're Selling And Making Sure They Buy It by Jeffrey Lant, JLA Publications, $30.00 postpaid. Write: Jeffrey Lant Associates, 50 Follen Street, Suite 507, Cambridge, MA 02138 or call (617) 547-6372. Ask for copy of the *Jeffrey Lant's Sure-Fire Business Success Catalog.* (Exhaustive study; reading the first chapter is worth buying the book, then pick and choose what is appropriate for you.)

OVERCOMING FEAR OF SELF-PROMOTION AND RISKING

The Psychology of Call Reluctance: How To Overcome the Fear Of Self-Promotion by George Dudley and Shannon Goodson, Behavioral Science Research Press, $18.95. (The first half of the book is a technical explanation of the different types of fear of self-promotion, the second half is strategies on how to get rid of the fears. Well written with a sense of humor, based on extensive research.)

Risking by David Viscott, M.D., Simon and Schuster, $3.95. (A fast reading "mini-manual" on the basics of successful risk taking.)

PERSONALITY PROFILING

Please Understand Me: Character & Temperament Types by David Keirsey and Marilyn Bates, Prometheus Nemesis Book Company, $9.95. (A well-written, easy-to-read study of sixteen personality types, much more in-depth than the Four-Quadrant approach. Includes a personality profile test with answer sheets for nine people and information on how your style relates to your values, your work, mating, children and leadership. This is excellent if you want to better understand your own motivations as well as others'. I recommend that you create your own profile by reading through all sixteen profiles and highlighting the qualities that you relate to *before you take the test.*)

THE ORIGINS OF EMOTIONAL BARRIERS

Bradshaw On: The Family - A Revolutionary Way of Self-Discovery by John Bradshaw, Health Communications, Inc., $9.95. (A very powerful and insightful book exposing the origins of emotional barriers as created by our family relationships. This is not light reading. To say this book is "revolutionary" is an understatement. You need to be ready for a big dose of reality. Read chapters 1-4 to understand the problem, then 9-11 to get the positive side. Then pick and choose through chapters 5-8 if you relate to the chapter headings.)

You Can Heal Your Life by Louise L. Hay, Hay House, $10.00. (Author of the bestselling book, *Heal Your Body*, and internationally known leader of the New Age Movement. The key message: "If you are willing to do the mental work, almost anything can be healed." She should know; she cured herself after being terminally diagnosed with cancer. Lots of easy-reading, practical information on healing old wounds--physical, mental, and emotional. Written from a metaphysical point of view.)

SPIRITUAL GROWTH

The Road Less Traveled: A New Psychology of Love, Traditional Values and Spiritual Growth by M. Scott Peck, M.D., Touchstone, $8.95. (Many people have read this book more than once cover to cover. A ton of useful information on personal growth issues. Start anywhere in the book.)

STRETCHING EXERCISES

Callanetics: 10 Years Younger in 10 Hours by Callan Pinckney, Avon, $9.95. Also available on videocassette by MCA Home Video. (Easy to do stretching exercises for maintaining body tone and great for getting the tension out of your body so you can better access your intuition.)

Sidney C. Walker

About the Author

Sid Walker is an expert on getting people to trust and act on "what feels intuitively right" in every aspect of their lives. Learning to listen to your intuition and risk following its advice is also what he calls "trusting yourself."

Over the past ten years, Sid has coached hundreds of business people on how to use their intuition to consistently make more profitable and personally satisfying decisions. His expertise has evolved from many years of "hands-on" experience as a peak performance coach working predominantly with top sales executives in the financial services field.

Sid is known for his extraordinary ability to help people identify the little things that make the difference between doing "okay" and "thriving." His specialty is creating methods for getting the most out of your natural strengths, or as he calls it, "staying on a roll."

Prior to embarking on his coaching career, Sid was a life insurance agent with Northwestern Mutual for four years, specializing in Disability Income Insurance. Academically, Sid has a multi-disciplinary Bachelor of Arts degree from Michigan State University emphasizing Management and Psychology.

The following is a partial list of the major companies represented by Sid's clients:

Acacia Mutual   Bankers Life and Casualty   Capitol Analysts
Christopher Weil & Co.   Connecticut Mutual   CIGNA
Equitable   Guardian Life   Guarantee Mutual   Great West Life
Integrated Resources   I.D.S. Financial Services
Century Companies   Manufacturers   Metropolitan
Monarch Life   Mutual of New York   National Life of Vermont
New England Life   Northwestern Mutual   Phoenix Mutual   Prudential
Security Life of Denver   State Mutual   Shearson Lehman Hutton
Arthur Young   Main-Hurdman   Touche Ross

FOR MORE INFORMATION ABOUT:

Individual Coaching Programs (in person or by telephone)

•

Seminar-Workshops for Agency or Company Meetings

•

Seminar-Workshops for Study Groups

•

Speaking Engagements

Contact:

Sid Walker
c/o High Plains Publishing Co.
900 Lincoln Station Box 300786
Denver, CO 80203

303/894-8237 (8-5 Mountain Time)

Order Form

To order copies of *Trusting YourSelf*, **copy** and complete this order form **or call 1-800-323-6567.** Colorado residents call **303-872-8906. Both numbers are 24-Hour Service.**

Price: $20.00 plus $3.00 shipping, allow 4-6 days for delivery in U.S.
(Colorado residents add 7.2% sales tax.)

Your Name _____

Company Name _____

Address _____

City_____State_____Zip _____

Country_____Daytime Telephone(___) _____

I want to send the book as a gift, please mail the book to:

Name_____

Address _____

City_____State_____Zip _____

A gift card will be enclosed from "Your Name" as stated above.

For **International Orders,** please make payment in U.S. dollars, specify "air" or "surface" mailing and include the appropriate postage for a 1 lb. 1 oz. package.

Payment Form:

❏ Check or Money Order Enclosed   Amount Enclosed $_____

❏ VISA/MasterCard #_____Exp. Date_____

Cardholder's Signature _____

Mail to: High Plains Publishing Co.
900 Lincoln Station Box 300786
Denver, CO 80203
(303) 894-8237 (8-5 Mountain Time)

Please call telephone numbers listed at the top of the page for book orders.